TWEEN
Spirituality

By Marcia Joslin Stoner

Offering Opportunities in Preteen Spiritual Growth

Abingdon Press

Tween Spirituality
Offering Opportunities in Preteen Spiritual Growth

ISBN 0-687-07551-3

Text credits are on p. 128.
Illustration Credits: p. 10: Dennis Jones, © 2001 Cokesbury; pp. 13, 15, 29: Barbara Upchurch, © 1995, 1998 Cokesbury;
p. 14: Randy Wollenmann, © 2002 Cokesbury; p. 43: Natalie Jaynes, © 2001 Cokesbury; pp. 48-49: Jack Kershner, © 2000 Cokesbury;
p. 61: Cheryl Mendenhall, © 2002 Cokesbury; p. 72: Charles Jakubowski, © 2002 Cokesbury; p. 77: Brenda Gilliam, © 2002 Cokesbury;
pp. 79-80: Susan Spellman, © 2002 Cokesbury; p. 85: John Robinson, © 2000 Cokesbury; p. 90: Brenda Gilliam, © 2000 Cokesbury;
p. 97: Megan Jeffery, © 2000 Cokesbury; p. 110: Nell Fisher, © 1995, 1998 Cokesbury; p. 119: Barbara Upchurch, © 1994, 1997 Cokesbury.
Photo Credits: cover, p. 28: Ron Benedict, © 2002 Cokesbury; all other photos courtesy of Photodisc.

03 04 05 06 07 08 09 10 11 12 — 10 9 8 7 6 5 4 3 2 1

MANUFACTURED IN THE UNITED STATES OF AMERICA

Table of Contents

108939

How to Use This Book

This book is separated into sections based on the areas in which a tween's church and family life intersect. However, the listing of activities within the categories of Sunday School, Other Church Settings, and Congregational Life are somewhat arbitrary. Choose activities from any category to fit the style of your particular church setting.

Enhance Your Existing Church Settings

Most of the activities in this book are meant as activities to expand and enhance what is already happening in the church setting. Pick and choose from these activities to help shift the emphasis of your tween's experiences to spiritual concerns.

Use as a Model

These activities are meant to be used as models for ways you can make spirituality a more intentional and central part of every action with tweens.

Articles

The articles for teachers, leaders, and congregations are meant to help your way of thinking about tweens and their spirituality. Use the articles as springboards for coming up with your own ideas; things to which you know your tweens will respond. Perhaps you're not sure to what your tweens will respond. Don't worry, you will quickly learn. Remember that some techniques must be practiced and become familiar before they are meaningful and appreciated. Don't reject a type of activity, such as quiet time, because your tweens (or even you) are uncomfortable with it. Continue for a quarter of the year. If at the end of a quarter you see no growth in this area, you will know that it is not reaching any of your tweens; but you might be surprised how familiarity often breeds comfort and enjoyment in some of your tweens.

Reproducible Family Section

The entire family section is reproducible. Since spirituality is about the whole life of a person, the family must be involved in helping create a spiritual atmosphere in order to foster a true spiritual life. Enlist the help of the parents. Parents truly want a spiritual life for their children, but often do not have the tools to help this happen. By giving them copies of the reproducible pages (pages 111-122), you will be giving them an opportunity to participate actively and effectively in the spiritual growth of their tween.

Tween Spirituality
(a lot more than worship)

Christianity is a lifelong relationship with God—a living, growing, changing relationship. It is a relationship that lasts this lifetime and beyond. It is a relationship that needs to be developed and nurtured in tweens.

Believe it or not, tweens are naturally spiritual beings. How do we nurture and encourage their budding spirituality?

- Involve tweens in spiritual disciplines—Bible study, prayer, corporate worship, journaling, and missions.
- Talk with your tweens. Ask them questions: What do the things you are studying or doing mean to you? How does it affect your relationship with God? How does it affect the way you live?
- Listen to your tweens. Let them ask you tough questions. Call in help when necessary to answer those questions.
- Let some questions go unanswered. Letting tweens speculate and work through some spiritual issues allows for greater spiritual maturity.
- Include some worship element in *every* event—even camping trips, pizza parties, and other special outings.
- Work with parents of tweens. Let them know what you are doing and ways they can guide their tweens spiritually.
- Be a mentor to your tweens and look for ways to informally introduce tweens to spiritual mentors. There are many formal programs that do this—and you should use these generously—but often the informal contacts with persons of faith have the greatest impact.
- Help develop spiritual disciplines in all tween leaders and teachers. They are the most likely mentors.
- Encourage tithing. Tithing is a spiritual activity. By tithing we give back to God, and that affects our relationship with God.
- Involve tweens in missions. Mission experiences help them carry spirituality into their everyday lives. With every mission project include Bible study, prayer, and journaling.
- Practice spiritual disciplines yourself. Tweens learn more from observation than from talk or assignments.
- Spirituality is time-consuming and requires PRACTICE, PRACTICE, PRACTICE! The rewards last through eternity.

Remember: Spirituality is about relationships—our relationships with each other, with God, and with everyone in the world.

Reproducible Pages for Tweens

Reproducible Pages for Families

Sunday School

Offering opportunities for spiritual growth should be central to the Sunday school experience of tweens.

Classroom Spirituality

- Make time for classroom worship every week (and make worship more than just a prayer).

  Have a set time and place for worship. (In a small room, that may mean you clear your table of all materials at the end of the session, and you put a Bible and cross in the middle of the table.)

- Find ways for tweens to help prepare and lead classroom worship experiences.

- Be creative; use many styles of worship.

- Even though you use many styles of worship, help tweens establish some worship traditions (such as prayer lists, moments of silence, sentence prayers, and so forth).

- Introduce tweens to prayer lists. (This can be very meaningful and the start of a lifelong practice.)
    - Use the prayer list for prayer during worship.
    - Have tweens make a copy of the prayer list for home use.
    - Keep your own prayer list of your tweens' needs and concerns, and use it daily to pray for your tweens.
  Caution: Don't let making a prayer list take too much time. Tweens will use this as a way to fill time.

- Introduce your tweens to spiritual journaling. (You will probably never know it, but for one or more of your tweens it may become one of their most powerful, lifelong spiritual disciplines.)

- Practice spiritual disciplines in the classroom. Bible reading, prayer, times of quiet listening to God—all of these help set habits that many of your tweens may carry through their entire lives.

- Practice spiritual discipline yourself. Even tweens and youth model behavior more than words. They also can spot a phony quickly. Practice yourself whatever you ask of your tweens.

- Work with the pastor, parents, and the worship committee to find truly meaningful ways for things tweens have done in the classroom to be used in the corporate worship service.

- Do missions with tweens. This helps them focus on people outside of themselves, and allows them to put their spirituality into practice by interacting with God's people and by giving of themselves, their money, their talents, and their time. Missions are a concrete expression of faith.

Note: Make photocopies of page 9 to give to all your tweens to hang up in their rooms as a personal reminder.

I Can Change the World

✴ Do a devotion daily.
✴ Read God's Word every day.
✴ Imitate Jesus.
✴ Learn all you can about being a disciple.
✴ Ask God for help.
✴ Attend worship regularly.
✴ Love one another.
✴ Challenge friends to follow with you.

Do all the good you can,
by all the means you can,
in all the ways you can,
in all the places you can,
at all the times you can,
to all the people you can,
as long as you ever can.

John Wesley's Rule

I can change the world because accepting Christ changes me.

Prayer

Prayer is essential to any life. Understanding prayer and practicing prayer in different ways is important to tweens. Use the activities in this section to study prayer.

A Cluster Diagram

You will need (for each group): large sheet of paper, marker, paper, pencils.

A cluster diagram is a visual way to explore something. Ask your tweens to create a cluster diagram about prayer. (This exercise can be done as a class or in small groups.)

As a model for the class or the small groups, on a large sheet of paper create a cluster diagram like the one on this page, leaving out the answers. (The answers listed are examples only.) Write the word *prayer* in the center. Draw six arrows out in all directions from the word. Write the words *Why?*, *Who?*, *What?*, *Where?*, *When?*, and *How?* at the end of the arrows, one word per arrow. Draw circles above or below each word. As the group(s) discuss prayer, they are to write answers in the circles.

Prayer List

You will need: paper, pencil.

Many churches have prayer groups and ongoing prayer lists, where the concerns and the joys for which the congregation is praying are listed. These lists are kept current, with new requests continually being added or past concerns being removed. Do a class prayer list. This allows tweens to voice some of their concerns. During each class worship, say a prayer for those people and concerns on the list.

A variation on the class prayer list is to allow each tween some time to write out his or her own list. Allow quiet time during each worship for the tweens to pray for their concerns.

Caution: Keep this activity to about five minutes in length; don't let it take over the entire session time.

Prayer Post

Give your room a special place around which to focus personal and class prayer time. One way to do this is with a prayer post. Invite tweens to create prayer lists that they will place on a group prayer post and use each session. Each week they may add items to the list or delete items from the list as situations change. Your tweens will add to the prayer post their individual prayer lists, so the size of your class will determine the height of your prayer post. Here are five options for preparing the prayer post. Let your tweens help stimulate your own creative approach!

1. Decorate a large cardboard wrapping paper tube and either mount it on a heavy cardboard base with masking tape so it can stand, or suspend it by strong wire from the ceiling. Glue clothespins to the tube—one per tween and teacher—to hold prayer lists.

2. Use an artificial Christmas tree as a "prayer pine" and use clothespins to hold prayer lists.

3. Use a section of one-inch PVC pipe for the post. On a twelve-inch square of plywood, mount a floor flange into which you will screw a male adapter that will hold the PVC pipe. A PVC cap on the top will finish it off neatly. These materials are all available where plumbing supplies are sold. If you wish, use gold spray paint to dress up the post and base. Add clothespins to the pipe.

4. Decorate a section of a bulletin board as your prayer post, providing pushpins to secure the tweens' prayer lists.

5. Use cardboard from a large appliance box or a foam core board available in office or art supply stores to construct a three-sided kiosk that will serve as your prayer post. If made large enough (each side at least twelve-inches wide), it should be freestanding and not require a base for stability. Using this option, create a prayer list "pocket" from construction paper for each tween and tape or glue it to the kiosk. Tweens can then easily remove their prayer lists each week and replace them when they are done.

Prayer Columns

You will need: four rectangular pieces of wood capable of standing alone, markers, napkin, cooking oil.

Use the ACTS (adoration, confession, thanksgiving, supplication) model of prayer to let your tweens make prayer columns from rectangular pieces of wood.

1. Have the tweens write a different ACTS word (*adoration, confession, thanksgiving, supplication*) on each piece of wood using felt-tip markers.

2. Let the tweens decorate the letters with additional colors.

3. When the letters are dry, have the tweens dip a napkin in cooking oil and rub the wood rectangle with the napkin to create a soft sheen.

Use the prayer columns in the classroom, or have your tweens make individual prayer columns to take home. Have the class compose an ACTS prayer and use the prayer columns on a regular basis to help remember this ACTS prayer.

Prayer Box

You will need: sturdy box with lid; cloth, clear adhesive paper, scraps of prepasted wallpaper, or gift-wrapping paper; knife (to make slit); pieces of paper; pencils; glue (if using cloth or wrapping paper).

To make a class prayer box, cover any sturdy box (with a lid) with cloth, clear self-adhesive paper, scraps of prepasted wallpaper, or gift-wrapping paper. Make a slit in the top of the box to allow tweens to put their prayer requests in the box. Sturdier boxes like shoeboxes last longer, but if you use a less durable box tweens can have the opportunity to decorate a new prayer box now and then.

Keep the prayer box on or near the worship table. Keep paper and a pen or pencil near the prayer box and encourage class members to write prayer requests on the paper and put them in the prayer box. Assure tweens that all prayer requests will be confidential, but anyone who wants the entire group to pray about something can tell the class his or her prayer request and put it in the box.

Be sure to pray a general prayer for all requests that have been put in the box.

Prayer Tree

You will need: bare branch or bush, large container filled with sand, construction paper, scissors, markers, glue, string (or yarn), paper clips.

Put a bare branch or a dead bush in a large container filled with sand. This is a prayer tree for your class.

1. Have each tween cut two circles out of construction paper (about 2½ inches across), then cut a slit in the circles from one point on the edge to the center.

2. Have the tweens decorate one side of the circle, then turn the circle over and write the name of the people or causes to pray for on the undecorated side.

3. Tell the tweens to overlap the two edges (decorated side out) at the slit to form a cone shape and glue the edges in place. (Use a paper clip to hold the edges together until the glue has dried completely.)

4. To finish the cones, have the tweens knot one end of a piece of string and insert it from the bottom inside of the cone through the top of the cone, pulling the string through until the knot rests under the center of the cone. Tie the string at the top into a loop. Hang "prayer request" cones on the tree.

   Note: If the cone is not tight enough to use knotted string, use yarn instead.

5. Have the tweens add cones to the prayer tree in future weeks instead of adding to a prayer list.

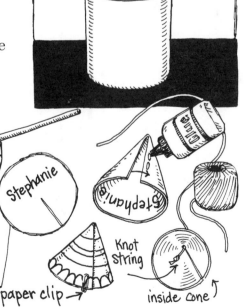

2½ inch circles

cut

Stephanie

paper clip →

Knot String

inside cone ↑

Prayer Chain

You will need: construction paper, scissors, markers, tape.

Have the tweens cut different colors of construction paper into long, narrow strips. Ask them to write one prayer request on each strip. Make circles (with the prayer request on the outside), looping each paper through another paper and taping the ends until they have created a paper chain. Have the tweens attach all of their chains together. Place this chain on the classroom altar. As the weeks go by, the chain will grow. Drape it around the room—walls, doorposts, everywhere. Each week pray for the concerns on the prayer chain. You might even have each tween select certain concerns from the chain to pray for each day during the week.

Cross Prayer Chain

You will need: construction paper, scissors, markers, tape.

During the Lenten-Easter season you may wish to add crosses to your paper prayer chain.

Have the tweens fold a piece of paper in half, then draw (or trace) a cross pattern onto the paper. Then have them cut out the cross, leaving it folded at the top so that you have a double-sided cross.

Ask the tweens to write one prayer request on the cross and then tape the bottom of the cross to the prayer chain. Have them repeat these steps for each of prayer requests. They may choose to use a different type of cross for each prayer request or the same type of cross for each, but use only one cross per request.

Prayer Braid

You will need: yarn, paper, marker.

To help your tweens with their own prayer time, encourage them to make a prayer braid. They can use the prayer braid to remind them each day of the things for which they want to pray.

1. Have the tweens write the name of someone or something they want to pray about regularly on a two- by one-inch piece of paper, then fold the paper in half lengthwise two times.

2. Ask them to take six twenty-inch strands of yarn, three strands each of two different colors.

3. Have them loop the yarn around a stable object with an open end, such as a doorknob or a chair post, with the middle of the yarn strands on the object. Then have them tie a knot to make a loop.

4. Tell the tweens to divide the strands into three groups, with each group made up of four strands, two of each color. Then have them begin braiding the yarn, treating each group of strands as one strand. Tell them to braid right over middle, left over middle, and so forth until you have braided one-half of the yarn.

5. Have the tweens place their folded paper on top of the middle strand, with the ends under each side strand.

6. Tell them to crisscross the outside strands over the paper and middle strand once and pull the yarn tight.

7. Tell the tweens to pull the middle strand to the front; and then loop it up, over, and behind the paper, bringing it forward below the paper.

8. Have the tweens tie the two side strands securely together under the middle strand, and let the strands hang as fringe.

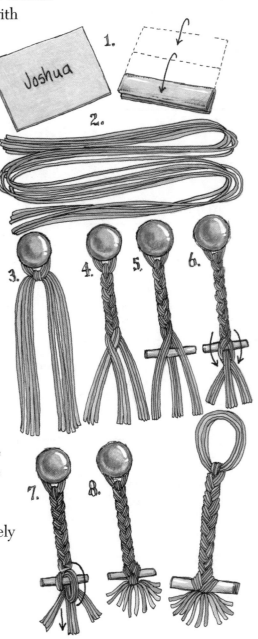

15

Prayer Doesn't Always Come Easy

You can pray anywhere, at any time, and you can say anything. But it's not always easy to pray. Write your responses on the chart below, putting harder stuff toward the left and easier stuff toward the right.

Places To Pray

Places Where It's Hard to Pray   Places Where It's Easy to Pray

Times To Pray

Times When It's Hard to Pray   Times When It's Easy to Pray

Things to Say

Things It's Hard to Say to God   Things It's Easy to Say to God.

Choose a Prayer Person

You will need: basket or bowl, paper, pencil.

To help your tweens understand intercessory prayer and its importance, have them choose a prayer person—a person they will pray for during the week. This person will be from their class and will be chosen by drawing a name.

Ask each of your tweens to write his or her name on a piece of paper and fold it. Place the papers in a basket or bowl and stir them up.

Ask each tween to draw a name out of the basket or bowl. (If a tween draws his or her own name, he or she is to refold it and place it back in the container.) The name each tween draws will be his or her "prayer person" for the week. He or she is to pray for this person every day of the week. If the tween has a normal prayer time, he or she will pray for the person during the normal prayer time. If the tween does not have a normal prayer time, ask him or her to choose a time and pray each day, including this person in his or her prayers.

This could be a one-time activity, or you could repeat this activity for several weeks, with the tweens drawing a different prayer person each week.

Note: If you think your tweens would be comfortable in doing so, encourage them to take a moment and ask their prayer partner if he or she has special prayer requests.

Use a Prayer Calendar

You will need: prayer calendar, or list of missionaries and a regular calendar.

A prayer calendar lists the names of all the missionaries a church has around the world, and the purpose is for people to pray for those missionaries. The calendar normally lists the missionaries by their birthdays. At least one denomination has a Children's Prayer Calendar that lists the children of missionaries. You can pray for these children, just as you do for the adults. Perhaps your denomination has calendars such as these.

If your denomination has a prayer calendar, get one for your class. If your church does not have a prayer calendar but you can get a list of missionaries, make your own prayer calendar.

Tweens may decide to pray for a missionary whose birthday is on the same date; or perhaps the class would like to look at a globe, select some locations around the world, and pray for missionaries in those areas.

Personal Prayer Books

You will need: small journals or supplies to make a prayer book (construction paper or heavy colored paper, white paper, markers, scissors, stapler and staples, ruler); pencils or pens; hymnals, books of prayers, books of worship, old curriculum student pieces, and anything else that contains appropriate prayers.

Explain to your tweens that it was a type of prayer when two blind men on the road shouted out to Jesus, "Lord, have mercy on us" (Matthew 20:29-30). All kinds of prayers are important in our lives. Sometimes it's difficult to get started on a prayer. Encourage your tweens to make their own prayer books that will help them in their personal prayer lives.

If you decide that they will make the books themselves instead of using purchased journals, do the following:

1. Let each tween decide how big he or she wants their book to be (one that fits in a pocket might be nice).

2. Have the tweens fold one sheet of white paper in half. (If they want to make the book smaller, use a ruler and pencil to mark the paper to the size they want it to be and cut the folded paper to fit that size.)

3. Let each tween decide how many pages he or she would like in his or her prayer book (for example, the book could have 8 pages, 12 pages, or 16 pages). Each folded sheet of white paper makes four pages for the book. Have the tweens fold as many pages of white paper as they need, cut them to the size they want, and then nest them together.

4. Have the tweens fold one sheet of construction paper or other heavy colored paper in half. (If they cut it, make sure it is slightly larger than the folded white sheets of paper.) Put this paper around the outside of the white pages.

5. Lay the books open and staple them two or three times in the crease where the paper was originally folded. Then fold the book closed again. The staples should hold the book together.

6. Encourage the tweens to decorate the cover any way they would like. Then have them write prayers and/or prayer helps in their prayer book to help them during their own private time.

Over the next few weeks have your tweens look at hymnals, books of prayers, books of worship, old pieces of tween curriculum, and any other material you might have that contains appropriate prayers. Let them choose which prayers speak to them and have them copy the prayers in their personal prayer books.

Ring a Bell for Prayer

You will need: hand bell, hand chime, or triangle.

Ask your tweens if they have ever noticed in your church the "chiming of the hour" at the beginning of the worship service (not all churches do this). Some churches actually ring a bell. This bell is calling people to worship. Many traditions use bells to call people to prayer services.

Ask your tweens to participate in a prayer where everyone will have an opportunity to mention someone or something for which they would like the class to pray during the week. Encourage them to speak briefly, to just say a name or one word. Remind others that during this time of prayer they should repeat the stated prayer to themselves.

Invite a participant to ring a hand bell, hand chime, or triangle after each request. You should start to provide the tweens with an example.

> You could say something like: **"Dear God, thank you for this day. Be with us during this time of prayer as we pray...for Latisha."** (The bell-ringer rings the bell.)
>
> The next person says another name, for example **"...for Michael."** (The bell-ringer rings the bell.)

You might want the class to sit in a circle. Not everyone needs to say something. As leader, you may close or ask someone else to close when you give an agreed-upon signal.

Sentence Prayers

During worship, invite your tweens to offer a sentence prayer (one sentence) about the particular topic the class has been studying. This works well if the tweens sit or stand in a circle and there is a signal for the next tween to start. (There is always someone who can't think of anything to say; he or she may say something like, "Thank you, God" or, "Be with us always." What they say depends upon the topic.)

Note: Holding hands and squeezing the hand of the next person is a good signal, but younger tweens often don't like to hold hands, and if they do, they sometimes use squeezing as a weapon. Know how your tweens will react before you actually use this method.

A Breath Prayer

Your class may want to experience a breath prayer. Invite the tweens to sit comfortably on the floor or in their chairs with their eyes closed while you play some instrumental music.

You will need to give your tweens some guidance. The following is a just a sample. Change the words according to that for which you are praying.

Take a deep, slow breath and think about the world around you.
Breathe out while saying, "We live in the world God created."
Take a deep, slow breath and think about how you are learning to be part of the church.
Breathe out while saying, "We believe God is the God of all."
Take a deep, slow breath and think about the people in your church.
Breathe out while saying, "We are called to be the church."
Take a deep, slow breath and think about how people show love to you.
Breathe out while saying, "We are called to work and serve others."
Say together, "God is with us always."

A Prayerful Cheer

You will need: large sheet of paper and marker or erasable board and erasable marker.

A breath prayer is quiet and introspective. A prayerful cheer is just the opposite: loud, boisterous, and joyful. A prayerful cheer can be used as a sending forth, a group benediction.

An example of this is the "One in Christ Cheer," which is listed below.

Have a leader read the lines in regular type and the rest of the group read the boldface type; or have one group read the regular type and the second group read the boldface type. Hold out the italicized words or syllables twice as long as the others so that the lines create a rhythm.

There *is* no longer Jew or Greek! **Jew or Greek!**
There *is* no longer slave or free! **Slave or free!**
There *is* no longer male or *fe*-male! **That's right!**
For *all* of you are one in Christ! **Amen!**

Print these words on a large sheet of paper or an erasable board for the class to read. (You can use different colors to indicate the different parts and the word emphasis.)

Guided Prayer

Guided prayer helps your tweens become more comfortable with silent prayer and helps them focus on specific needs and concerns. In guided prayer always pause between instructions to allow those in prayer time to adequately pray. These examples are to help you become acquainted with how to use guided prayer. Once you become comfortable with the method, do your own guided prayer whenever you feel it is appropriate for worship with your tweens.

Guided Prayer 1—Asking for Forgiveness

This guided prayer will help your tweens ask for forgiveness.

> **Say: Close your eyes and think about how much God loves you. Silently thank God for that love.**
>
> **Think about a time when you have done something that God would not want you to do. Remember how you felt. Ask God now for forgiveness.**
>
> **Think again about how much God loves you. Silently thank God for that love.**

Guided Prayer 2—Bread

In any session where you are talking about bread (when topics are Communion, world hunger, Jesus as the bread of life, the loaves and the fishes, and so forth), you might use the following guided prayer.

Have various kinds of bread in the worship center (crackers, pita bread, tortillas, wheat bread, and so forth). Ask each tween to choose one piece of bread from the tray and, while they eat in silence, have them pray the following prayer (pausing for silent responses).

> **Holy God, we pray for people who hunger for food.**
> **And we pray for people who have more food than they need.**
> **We pray for people who hunger to learn your ways.**
> **And we pray for those who never think, "What would Jesus do?"**
> **We pray for people who are sick and need your healing touch.**
> **And we pray for people who are healthy, happy, and those who are celebrating special events.**
> **Amen.**

Guided Prayer 3—Love One Another

Ask each tween to sit with feet on the floor and hands in his or her lap. Have them close their eyes. Speak these statements in a quiet but firm voice. Pause after each statement.

Pray in thanksgiving for the times in this class when you have felt loved. *Take a deep breath. Exhale very slowly. Take another deep breath. Exhale slowly.* **Pray for strength to endure those times when you do not feel loved in this class.** *Take a deep breath. Exhale very slowly. Take another deep breath. Exhale slowly.* **Pray for help to always be loving to each one in the class.** *Take a deep breath. Exhale very slowly. Take another deep breath. Exhale slowly.* **Think about a time when you have disobeyed Jesus' command to love one another. How did you feel? How do you think the other person felt? Pray for help to do better in loving others at all times. Amen.**

Guided Prayer 4—In Prison

This guided prayer is meant to be used when studying Peter in prison. It could be adapted for use when you are studying Paul.

Ask everyone to sit quietly with closed eyes. Ask them to breathe in deeply, then out deeply. Have them practice this breathing several times. Read the following prayer, pausing where appropriate to allow for silent reflection. Your voice should be calm but not monotonous.

Say: Think about Peter in his prison cell. It is very dark. There is only one oil lamp on the rock walls. See the guards around Peter, feel the weight of his chains on your arms and legs. Hear the muffled cries of other prisoners in nearby cells. Hear the dogs bark on the street outside. Smell the dirt floor and the smoke from the lamp. Feel the dampness and chill of the air coming off the Mediterranean Sea. The cold rock chills you to the bone. Imagine what is going through Peter's mind. Remember the fearful night when Jesus was arrested. Then remember the amazing things that have happened since—the Resurrection, the coming of the Holy Spirit—and how he was no longer afraid. But that fear is now creeping back.

Now remember a time when <u>you</u> were very afraid. Maybe you found yourself in over your head at the swimming pool. Maybe you were lost. Maybe someone was very angry with you, or maybe it was the day the World Trade Center was attacked.

Now see the light come into Peter's cell. Imagine his joy, his relief, his praises for God. Allow that same light to come into your own fearful place. Imagine it surrounding you, protecting you. Feel the touch of God's love. Feel God's presence all around you. Know that God is with you right now, loving you.

Breathe in deeply. Breathe out. Breathe in again. Slowly, when you are ready, open your eyes.

Silence

In modern society silence is underrated. We watch television and read at the same time. We play music and work on the computer while we talk to whoever is in the room. We multi-task for everything. Modern worship has become hyperactive using video, overhead projectors, contemporary music, and a lot of movement to keep our attention. Even in many traditional worship services, silent prayer has fallen out of use.

When do we keep silent? When do we refresh ourselves from all the hustle and bustle? When do we listen to God?

We cannot even think of silence and tweens in the same sentence. If tweens are silent it's usually because they are sleeping, bored, or pouting about something. However, with practice tweens can become comfortable with, and even appreciative of, silence.

Silent Prayer

Have a time of silent prayer with your tweens on a regular basis. Start with thirty seconds, work up to a minute, and then to a minute and a half (two minutes is about their limit). At first your tweens will be uncomfortable (just as adults are). But have a time of silent prayer every session for a quarter, and you will see the comfort level and the ability to be quiet increase. Resist the urge to guide them. (Guided prayer is wonderful and appropriate, but time to develop our own unfettered relationship with God is also important.)

You cannot force tweens (or anyone else) to pray or listen for the Word of God during a moment of silence, but you can provide them with the opportunity for the wonderful silence in which to let the Holy Spirit do its work.

Silent Meditation

Practice Christian meditation with your tweens, either prior to or in place of part of the worship time. Some tweens may have heard that, because meditation is also practiced by people of other faiths, or by people of no faith at all, Christians should not practice it. You can respond that the practice of Christian meditation goes back to at least the third century. When Christians practice meditation, they do so in order to know the presence of God proclaimed by, and incarnated in, Jesus Christ.

Ask the tweens to sit separately around the room or area. Make the room as quiet as possible. Separating the tweens allows them to develop their own quiet place.

Ask everyone to close their eyes and breath deeply. Have them take a deep breath and then very slowly exhale. Have them do this again, only every time they exhale have them repeat, "Jesus Christ, Giver of the Spirit, lead my life" over and over. Do this meditation for about two minutes. The first time you do this exercise, two minutes will seem forever. However, with practice Christian meditation may become the favorite exercise of some of your tweens. Remember, the Holy Spirit can come to us at anytime, and that includes in the silence.

Silent Center

You will need: items of your choice.

Instead of starting each class with a rowdy activity, for a few weeks begin with a "silent center." Most of us are familiar with learning centers, where tweens work in different areas with different types of learning experiences. A silent center is just another type of learning area. It can also be done in a regular classroom setting with the silent center as the opening activity.

To make an effective silent center, set up a worship table and each week add or change items on the table, depending upon what you are studying. Have your tweens study the center for one minute in silence, looking at what is there. At the end of one minute ask questions about what they see on the worship table or how they feel about what they have seen and heard. (Use this worship table again at the closing worship to tie the class time together.)

For example: During the Advent and Christmas seasons, have an open Bible (change it to a different Bible reference each week), an Advent wreath (add one candle per week, and light the candle during the actual worship experience), and a Christmas ornament signifying which part of the Christmas story is being experienced that week. You can either add an ornament each week or change the ornament each week. After your time in the silent center, ask the tweens what each item signifies, but also what new things they see.

Another example: If you are studying the story of Moses and the burning bush, you might have an open Bible, a candle, a pair of sandals, and some leaves representing the bush. Ask your tweens what these items represent.

Silence/Moving/Breathing

You will need: cassette/CD with music of hymns, cassette/CD player.

Silence does not always mean sitting perfectly still. To engage the class—and especially your physical learners—begin with a breathing/movement exercise. Play hymns such as "Let All Mortal Flesh Keep Silence" or "Star-Child." (Check with your music director for a hymn or song with the same tempo if you do not have these on a cassette or CD.)

Song 1 option—"Let All Mortal Flesh Keep Silence": Ask everyone to squat down and assume a "completely deflated balloon" position on the floor. As the music begins, they are to inhale slowly and "inflate" through the line, "for with blessing in his hand" (eleven measures), at which point they should be standing straight up, on their toes, arms fully extended overhead, their lungs full of air. As the line, "Christ our God to earth descendeth…" is sung, they begin to "deflate," slowly exhaling and returning to their original position (in seven measures). Repeat with verses 2 through 4.

Song 2 option—"Star-Child": Again start by squatting down in the "completely deflated balloon" position. As the music begins, they inhale and "inflate" through the line, "heaven's lightening rod" (eight measures). As the line, "this year, this year…" is sung, they begin to "deflate" to their original position (in seven measures). Repeat with verses 2 through 5.

The Potter

You will need: cassette/CD player, cassette/CD with the music to the hymn "Have Thine Own Way, Lord" (or perhaps the church musician would record a version for your use), modeling clay.

As the music begins, ask your tweens to think silently about the areas that need to be reshaped or remolded in their lives. Give each tween a small portion of clay and ask him or her to softly and quietly work the clay in his or her hands, experiencing the power to mold and shape the clay as God has the power to mold and shape each of them.

Tell the tweens to imagine how God looks at each of us. From the moment of our birth we have been shaped, reshaped, molded, and refined to be the person we are today, the person who God wants us to become. We know how God wants us to live, and it is up to us to do it. Talk about how we sometimes make poor choices and fail to do what God wants us to do, but God does not discard us as scraps. God continues to love and care for us. God continues to call us to become all we are meant to be.

Together pray the following litany prayer:
For families who mold us with their love and care,
Have thine own way, Lord.
For those who mold us by living a Christian example,
Have thine own way, Lord.
For your Word that guides and shapes us day to day,
Have thine own way, Lord.

Alone Time

Encourage your tweens to explore their spiritual lives on their own time. Give a copy of the following to your tweens.

CUT ALONG DOTTED LINE ➘

Sabbath—Time for You/Time for God

Sabbath is a time of rest. The first mention of the idea of the sabbath is in Genesis 2:1-3. On the seventh day of Creation, God rested. In Exodus 20:8-11, the fourth commandment is to rest on the sabbath. Leviticus 25:1-7 says that God told the Israelites through Moses that they were to let the land rest for one year out of every seven.

Just as the sabbath rest for the land gave it time to renew itself so that it could be more productive, a sabbath rest gives us time to reenergize ourselves. In order to be productive and healthy, our bodies, minds, and souls need time to rest and relax. Here are some ideas to help you create some sabbath time for yourself each week.

* Find a quiet place, perhaps somewhere outside. Sit quietly, breathing deeply, for five minutes. Let your mind wander. (This is great for your imagination.)

* Choose one of your favorite Bible verses. Whenever you have to wait for something, say this verse over and over to yourself.

* Listen to Christian music.

* Watch a sunset.

* At the end of the day, remember all the good things that have happened to you during the day.

* Sit quietly. Imagine all the muscles in your body relaxing one by one. Breathe deeply and slowly ten times.

* Read a psalm from the Bible.

* Pray a listening prayer. Sit quietly, listening for God rather than telling God things.

* Take a walk. Look for beautiful things in God's world.

* Read a book for the sheer joy of it. Thank God for books and for the time to enjoy them.

Classroom Worship

Worship in your classroom or any other setting should be very important—not just a quick prayer as an afterthought. Whether time-consuming or very short, make worship special.

Use Candles

Tweens (like many of us) love candles. They especially like to light (and to extinguish) the candle or candles on the worship table. Light one or more candle(s) for each worship. Allow the tweens to take turns lighting and extinguishing the candle(s).

Important: Whenever you light candles, make sure you supervise the tweens and that you have water available to extinguish any flames if necessary.

Make Candles

You will need: Old newspapers, wax-coated paper cups or plastic yogurt containers, candle wicks, sticks or pencils, pan of hot water, hot plate or stove, paraffin wax, can, old crayons, funnel.

Cover a work area with several layers of newspaper. Give each tween a wax-coated paper cup or plastic yogurt container. If the container is not wax-coated, have the tweens rub the inside of the container with cooking oil.

Have each tween cut a length of candle wick (as long as the container is tall, plus two inches), then tie one end of the wick onto a stick or unsharpened pencil. Lay the stick across the top of the container so that the wick hangs into the middle of the container.

Place a pan of water on a hot plate or stove. Put paraffin wax in a can. Set the can of paraffin in the pan of hot water to melt. (This makes a double boiler.) Melt enough paraffin so that the can is about three-fourths full. Add crayons (with paper removed) to color the wax. You may want to have several cans of paraffin heating in order to have more than one color for layering.

Have an adult use a funnel to pour the hot paraffin into the containers. Let the paraffin cool. Have the tweens cut off the wicks and tear off the container when the wax has hardened.

Make Candleholders

You will need: old newspapers, empty plastic bottles, sand, paper, white glue, water, paper cups, brushes, colored tissue paper, candles.

Important: Make sure and exercise caution when using these candleholders and candles. Never leave lit candles unattended.

Spread out old newspapers to protect the table. Choose empty plastic bottles to use for the candleholders—the necks are a perfect size for holding a candle.

Have the tweens make a mixture of white glue and a little water in a paper cup. Holding the bottle with their finger in the opening, have them apply the glue and water mixture with a brush all over the bottle—except for the bottom. Then, have them take pieces of tissue paper—cut or torn into a variety of shapes and sizes—and place them all over the bottle. Let the tissue pieces overlap, and have them continue brushing on more diluted glue. (If you are completing this activity near the Advent season, use Advent colors—purple, blue, or red, with some white for contrast. Wrinkles are fine—it doesn't have to be smooth. Texture is kind-of cool.) When the bottle is covered, have the tweens brush on a few more layers of the glue. It takes time for the candleholder to dry. You might want to make these during one class for use at the next session so that the candleholders will be dry.

After the glue has dried, make a funnel from a sheet of paper and fill the bottle about halfway full with sand—just enough to make it stable. Put in your candle, and you're ready to go!

Put all of the candleholders and candles on your worship table. Allow a time at the beginning of worship for each tween to light his or her candle and pray silently. As each candle is lit the worship table will make quite a statement.

Worship Experiences

Add any of the special worship experiences on the following pages to your regular classroom worship format. These are not full worship experiences, but they have the central worship element.

Worship: Repentance

You will need: old shirts, one coffee can, masking tape, brown liquid shoe polish or black or brown crayons or felt-tip markers, paper towels, sand, slips of paper, pencils, matches, glass of water.

Your tweens will need to wear old shirts over their clothes. Have them tear off short pieces of masking tape and completely cover the coffee can with the tape, overlapping the edges.

Have them use the applicators that come with the shoe polish to wipe the polish all over the tape. Use paper towels to wipe off the excess shoe polish. This will give the can an old leather look. Or, you can let the tweens rub over the tape with the sides of black or brown crayons or with felt-tip markers.

Pour a small amount of sand in the bottom of the can. Set the finished can in the worship area.

Pass out slips of paper and ask your tweens to think about of what they need to "repent", or for what they need to ask forgiveness, and to write these on the slips of paper you have given them—one per paper. Assure them that no one else will see these. When they have finished have them put their slips of paper in the can.

Pray: God, we are sorry for the times we have acted in unloving ways toward our neighbors. Forgive us for the times we have hurt someone else. Let these burning slips of paper represent your forgiveness and our renewed commitment to love you and our neighbors.

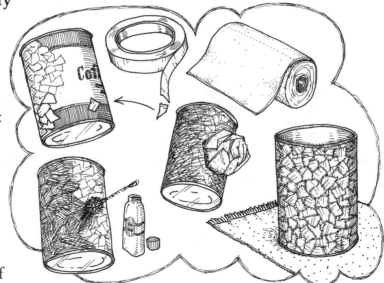

As you pray, light the slips of paper that the tweens put in the can, and let them burn (in the can). Keep a glass of water on hand in case the fire should become too large. Make sure that the fire is completely out at the end of your worship.

Worship: Remembering Flames

You will need: candle for worship table, one candle with drip protector, matches.

When talking about the story of Timothy or at any time when you are discussing passing on the faith (especially from one generation to another), you might want to use this activity for worship.

Have your tweens stand or sit in a circle. Light the candle that sits on the worship table.

Ask: Who first told you about God? How did he or she do that? (Allow time for discussion.) **We learn so many things from our families, so it's not surprising that we learn about God from our families. Those who have experienced God before us pass their faith onto us.**

Light the candle with a drip protector from the candle on the worship table.

Talk about how sometimes people use the phrase "passing the torch" to talk about the way each generation gives its knowledge and gifts to the coming generations. The faith we have is indeed like a light that is passed to us from all those who have carefully watched over the faith in their own lives. Tell them this candle symbolizes the light that comes to us from those who have gone before us, and that they are to pass the candle completely around the class without the flame going out. (Pass the candle around the circle once.)

Say: Faith is like a flame. We must carefully keep watch over it until it has reached the hands of the next generation. (Let the tweens pass the flame again if they are interested in doing so.)

End with a prayer for all of those who have gone before and for all of those who will come after. Carefully extinguish the candle.

Worship: Least of These

You will need: candle for worship table, one candle with drip protector per tween, matches.

Gather the class together at your worship center. Read Matthew 25:34-40. Have each tween light his or her candle (with drip protector) and name a way in which he or she has done something for "the least of these," saying:

Lord, I saw you _____ (hungry, thirsty, a stranger, naked, sick, in prison, lonely, depressed, frightened, etc.) **and I _____** (helped organize a food drive, stayed until the police arrived, bundled up the clothes I had outgrown and delivered them to Goodwill Industries, and so forth)**.**

Lead the class in reading Matthew 25:40 together.

Worship: Blessings

Explain to your tweens that many times when we pray, it is to ask God for something. It is called a "petitionary prayer"; that is, we are petitioning God for help. A petitionary prayer is a good thing, but it is also important to remember how blessed we already are, and how much we have already received.

Explain that today you are going to take turns giving God thanks for blessings. As the class leader you should begin. Give your tweens the option of saying their prayer aloud or saying "Amen" if they do not wish to pray aloud. (Saying "Amen" would then be the signal for the next tween to begin his or her prayer.)

At the end of their prayers, pray an individual blessing for each of your tweens. You may offer your own blessing for each tween, or use this traditional blessing from Numbers 6:24-26:

> **Pray:** (Name), **the LORD bless you and keep you; the LORD make his face to shine upon you, and be gracious to you; the LORD lift up his countenance upon you, and give you peace.**

Worship: Creation

This is a worship activity you might want to use when you study Creation.

Take your tweens outside of the church building. This exercise is to be done individually and in silence. Give them a time limit (such as five or ten minutes, depending upon the area you have) to take a walk around the immediate area. They are to look at God's creation and discover something that they would like to place on the worship table.

When they return to the classroom, ask each tween to place his or her item on the worship table and explain why he or she chose the item. How does it show God's great creation?

Variation: Do the walk exactly as above, but when they return, divide them into teams. Have each team "make" something using all of the things brought in as their contribution to worship. Give them fifteen or twenty minutes to do so. At the end of the time let each group present their creations, and explain why they chose the items they did and what their creation means.

Worship: Put God First

You will need: two identical pitchers, tennis ball, sand.

Ask for a volunteer to read Deuteronomy 6:4.

Have two identical pitchers (one empty and one filled with dry sand) and a tennis ball sitting before you on a table.

Slowly pour the sand into the empty pitcher as you say: **We all want to have nice things. We want to live in nice houses. We want to have our own bedrooms with beautiful furniture, nice carpet, and lots of electronic gadgets. We want to attend good schools and make good grades, so that we can get into a good profession. We want to wear the latest styles in clothes; to participate in sports; to take dance lessons, or piano lessons, or acting lessons. We want to have wonderful things and no worries. We want to be very, very happy.** (By now, the sand should have filled the pitcher completely.)

Continue saying: **Oh, yes, we also want to worship God. We want to love God with heart, soul, strength, and mind.** (Pick up the ball and place it on top of the sand.) **But often we spend all our time, our energy, and our money getting "things" and we forget to take time to love and worship God. Taking time for God just does not fit into our busy lives.**

Continue saying: **But** (place the ball in the newly emptied pitcher) **when we remember to put God first,** (begin pouring sand around the ball) **we find that a wonderful thing happens. We still want good schools and electronic gadgets. We still want to play sports, or to take music lessons. We still want to be happy. And, because we began by putting God first, we find time and energy and money to do the things that are really important to God and to us.**

They will see that the ball and all the sand fit into the pitcher. Resist the temptation to explain the moral of this exercise or to talk about scientific principles. Just remain silent for a moment and let the visual speak for itself.

Worship: World Communion Sunday

Before your class worship arrange with two good readers to read the Bible verses. To open worship have the first reader read Matthew 26:26-30 aloud and the second reader read John 13:34-35 aloud.

Tell the tweens that according to John's Gospel, on the night before Jesus died, Jesus reminded the first disciples to love one another just as he had loved them. As disciples of Jesus, we can depend on one another. Go on to explain that if they trust and depend on one another they can accomplish a "circle sit."

Have everyone stand in a circle, with each tween turned sideways so that he or she is facing the back of the next tween. They should be about two feet apart. Have each tween reach out and place his or her hands on the shoulders of the person in front of him or her.

Tell the tweens that each person will have to trust the person in back of him or her, and that they must work together or no one will succeed. At your signal ("sit") they are to sit down very carefully, as though there were chairs behind them. Their hands will have to remain on the shoulders of the person in front of them as this will help guide that person. If everyone sits correctly, each person will be sitting comfortably on the knees of the person behind them.

After they have successfully completed the circle sit, have everyone sit in a regular circle on the floor and discuss the experience. Ask them how it felt to know that another person was helping them. Ask how it felt to help someone else.

After the discussion have everyone close their eyes.

Say: Imagine that every Christian in every country of the world is standing in a circle, ready to support others and ready to be supported by others. Imagine Jesus standing in the middle of the circle, breaking bread and offering it to everyone in the circle. Now imagine a worldwide circle sit. Every Christian in every country is supporting someone else and is being supported by someone else. Imagine that every Christian is able to reach out with one hand and accept the bread from Jesus while still sitting on the knees of another Christian. Today is World Communion Sunday. Today disciples of Jesus are participating in Holy Communion services in churches around the globe. Today Christians in every country are remembering how much God loves us. Today Christians are remembering that we are to love one another.

Close with prayer, giving thanks for Jesus' life, death, and resurrection, and giving thanks for disciples of Jesus, who love one another.

Worship: Water and the Drop of Red

You will need: Bibles, white toilet paper or white paper towels or tissue paper cut into 3- by 3-inch sections, glass of clear water, medicine dropper, red food coloring.

This activity is meant to be incorporated into a Pentecost worship experience.

Your tweens will need to be at a table, but close enough to you so that you can easily reach each persons' paper. Place a glass of water in the middle of the table where it is clearly visible to all. Distribute one of the following to the class members: one section from a roll of white toilet tissue; a piece of white paper towel cut into 3- by 3-inch squares, or white tissue paper cut into 3- by 3-inch sections. (You want them to be able to divide the paper into four equal sections.)

Ask the tweens to take a marker and draw lines dividing their paper into four sections. Have them label their sections "self," "family," "friends," and "school." When they have finished, have them place their paper on the table in front of them.

Say: **The water represents us; all the things that make us who we are—the way we talk and act, the way we have fun, the persons we have come to be.**

Fill a medicine dropper with clear water from the glass. Read the following and after each statement squeeze one drop of water into the appropriate section of each tween's tissue.

Say: **We live as individuals. We live in families. We have friends. We attend school. In all of these places we have relationships and familiar patterns and ways of doing things.**

Say: **Suppose we start a relationship with God. We begin to trust Jesus. We start to have real faith in everything Jesus said and did. What does the Bible say happens when we trust Jesus?**

Have one tween read Ephesians 3:16-17 and another read Philippians 2:5. Pour some of the red food coloring into the glass of water, then fill the medicine dropper again. Again, after each comment put a drop of red water onto the appropriate square.

Say: **Remember the story of the Holy Spirit coming at Pentecost? When we trust in Jesus, Jesus comes to us. We still have our lives. We still live as individuals. We still live in families. We still have friends. We still attend school. But what happened to the water? What happens to our lives?** (they are the same, but they look different)

Worship: Rebuilding Mosaic

You will need: construction paper, markers, posterboard, pencil, glue.

Give each tween a piece of construction paper—hand out a variety of colors—and ask him or her to draw and color a biblical symbol on the paper (such as the wise men's star, the fish, Jacob's ladder, or a lamb).

When the tweens have finished their pictures, tell them to think about something they have done wrong or feel regret for saying or doing. They are not to say this out loud, just to think about it. After a minute of silence ask them to take the picture they made and tear it into pieces. Tell them that this action symbolizes what happens when we sin against God. It separates us; it tears us apart from God and others.

Now tell them that they are going to take these torn papers and make them into a mosaic of a new symbol. Have the class decide upon a new symbol. (A cross or a rainbow might be appropriate, but it does not have to be an already-recognized symbol. Strongly encourage creativity.) Encourage discussion about what the symbol should be and why.

On a piece of posterboard let a volunteer sketch in pencil the new chosen symbol. Have another volunteer outline the symbol with black felt-tip marker. Then have the entire class take the pieces of their individual artwork and glue them onto the new symbol in a mosaic pattern.

Tell the group that while separation tears us apart, forgiveness can bring us together again, but things will never look the same. Depending upon our acceptance of forgiveness, sometimes we can make something even better than before.

Have them post their new symbol in your worship area and use it as the centerpiece for your worship.

Note: Some tweens will love tearing up their work; others may find it traumatizing. Assure any tween who is reluctant that their picture will be used to make something even better. If anyone is still reluctant to tear up their work, let them keep their picture and ask them to do another one to be torn up.

Litanies

A litany is a group prayer. Tweens like to participate, but sometimes they are not very good at it. Litanies give them a chance to participate. Have the group practice before doing any litanies, even for classroom worship. Always have some or all of the tweens stand to do litanies. Standing gives the impression of the litany being more than a reading assignment. Sometimes dividing up litany assignments as in the sample below creates more interest.

Jesus Said...
(A Litany Based on Luke 6:32-35)

Reader One: And Jesus told the people these things…
Reader Two: If you love those who love you,
ALL: What's so special about that?
Reader Three: Even sinners love those who love them.
Reader Four: If you do good to those who do good to you,
ALL: What's so special about that?
Reader One: For even sinners are good to people who treat them right.
Reader Two: If you loan something to someone, hoping to receive something in return,
ALL: What's so special about that?
Reader Three: Even sinners loan to others to get something they want.
Reader Four: Do good to others, expecting nothing in return.
ALL: Love one another as God loves you. And you will be children of the light!
Reader Two: Forgiving those who hurt you,
Reader Three: Giving to those who take from you, and
Reader Four: Treating others as you would like to be treated.
ALL: That's a special kind of love. That's the love that comes from God.

An Impossible Litany (Based on Luke 1:37)

Have fun with litanies. They are a great way to learn a Bible verse. Have the tweens try this one or take a Bible verse and try writing their own Bible verse litany.

Leader: For nothing,
ALL: nothing,
Leader: For nothing,
ALL: nothing, nothing, nothing, nothing, absolutely nothing
Leader: will be impossible
ALL: will be impossible,
Leader: nothing,
ALL: nothing,
Leader: nothing,
ALL: nothing,
Leader: will be impossible,
ALL: will be impossible,
Leader: with God,
ALL: with God,
Leader: nothing impossible
ALL: impossible with God.
Leader: Possible!
ALL: Possible!
Leader: Everything!
ALL: Possible!
Leader: For nothing will be impossible.
ALL: Nothing?
Leader: Nothing!
ALL: Nothing?
Leader: Nothing!
ALL: For nothing will be impossible with God!
ALL: For nothing will be impossible with God!

Write a Litany—1

You will need: index cards and pens or pencils, large sheet of paper, markers.

Your tweens will love writing litanies if they are going to actually be used in worship. You can use their litanies in classroom worship; check with your pastor about the possibility of using them in congregational worship as well.

Explain to your tweens that the reader will read some of the lines and the congregation will respond with lines written for them or with a recurring line. (Using a verse from a psalm as the recurring response is an easy method to find an appropriate response line.)

The following instructions are written using Psalm 107:1 as the response line, but the instructions are only an example of the method. Adapt them to suit whatever you are studying.

Step 1.
> **Say: Often when we think about gifts God has given us, we think about God's creation of the world. We think about the beauty of nature—that plants and animals provide us food; that sun, soil, and water sustain life. But one of God's greatest gifts is the gift of relationships. The prophets warned the people of Israel that they were breaking their relationship with God when they worshiped other gods and when they treated their neighbors unjustly.**

Step 2. Give each tween a three-by-five index card.
> **Say: The Bible is the story of God's continuing relationship with people. Recall one of your favorite Bible stories and think about God's actions in that story. Write on your card something about that story and the gift God gave in that story.**

Step 3. Collect all the cards and help the tweens arrange the cards into an appropriate sequence. Help the class refine the way the cards fit together. Let a volunteer write the litany on a large sheet of paper, remembering to add the response line (Psalm 107:1). (Or, if you have arranged with the pastor ahead of time, have them write it on a sheet of paper and give it to the church secretary for printing in the church worship bulletin.) Let the class be the leaders and the congregation the responders for the litany reading.

This specific litany may help your tweens recognize the Bible as a record of God's actions, of God's continuing faithfulness to a wayward people. This litany-writing activity may help your tweens begin to analyze favorite Bible stories. They may glean new meaning from a familiar story.

Write a Litany—2

You will need: large sheet of paper, markers.

For those who have never done any work writing a litany of their own, try the following method to get the class started. On a large sheet of paper write, "Blessed is the one who comes in the name of the Lord" four times, leaving a large space to write between each of the first three times it is written.

See below what your tweens are to write after each of the first three lines. Ask each tween to write one or more names below each line. This may become a group activity by allowing groups to work together to make their own form of this litany.

Blessed is the one who comes in the name of the Lord!
(Write the names of teachers, ministers, choir leaders and members, ushers, and greeters.)
Blessed is the one who comes in the name of the Lord!
(Write the names of people who help those who are hungry, sick, worried, or friendless. Write the names of those who preach, who pray, and who go on mission trips.)
Blessed is the one who comes in the name of the Lord!
(Write the names of people who have shown love to you.)
Blessed is the one who comes in the name of the Lord!

Write a Galatians 6:10 Litany

You will need: Bibles, paper, pencils.

For your tweens' next step in the process of litany-writing, choose a Bible verse and have the class work as a group to write a litany like the one below that is based on Galatians 6:10. The Bible verse could be divided into sections, with responses inserted between the sections. Encourage creativity.

For example:

Leader: Whenever we
Response: All, everybody, every one of us
Leader: have an opportunity,
Response: a chance, a time and a way to do something
Leader: Let us
Response: We, Juaquin, Michael, Belinda, Amanda, and Maria, not someone else.
Leader: Work for the good of all....

Bible Study

Bible study is essential to any Christian life. Tweens need Bible study, but they need Bible study that has relevance to their lives and that helps them explore for themselves what they believe.

The Bible and Tween Issues

You will need: Bibles.

Help your tweens understand that the Bible is relevant to the lives they live not just on Sunday but also on Monday through Saturday.

The following are just a few samples of some of the issues the Bible can help your tweens deal with:

1. Friendship—Use the New Testament to explore the nature of friendship with your tweens. Some of the friendships you can study are: the friendship of Mary, Martha, and Lazarus with Jesus; the twelve disciples—their relationships with each other and with Jesus; John, the disciple Jesus loved (best friend?); Paul and Barnabas; and Timothy and Paul. Also look at the friendship of the four friends who lowered their paralytic friend through the roof to Jesus (Mark 2:1-12).

2. Sibling Rivalry—Look at the stories of Cain and Abel, Jacob and Esau, and Joseph and his brothers. What's wrong with these pictures? What happens when jealously and anger get out of hand? How could things have been handled differently? Also look at the final reconciliation of Jacob and Esau and Joseph and his brothers. Look at the relationship of Mary and Martha to their brother Lazarus (a more positive role model, although Mary and Martha do have a little go-round when Jesus visits).

3. Guidance for everyday life. Have them look at some of these Bible verses: Proverbs 19:17; Matthew 5:8, 6:19-21, 7:12; Luke 6:37-38, 45; John 14:1; 1 Corinthians 13; Galatians 5:22-26; and 1 Thessalonians 5:11. (If you think about it, you probably already know other Bible verses that can be used to help tweens with their everyday choices and living.)

Every week give some Bible study time to an issue that effects your tweens. Let your curriculum be your guide—everything in the Bible is relevant—but also get to know something about the lives of your tweens. Be flexible. If something seems to strike a chord or they want to talk more about a topic, let them. In matters of faith, curriculum is a guide, not a school lesson with subject matter to be tested at the end of the year. Let the Holy Spirit work through you and your time together to help your tweens explore their faith, and they will discover that it is very relevant to their lives.

Who Do You Say I Am?

Help your tweens begin their journey of making their faith their own by helping them think through what they really believe about Jesus.

Ask your tweens to think about what some people they know might say to the question if Jesus asked today, "Who do you say I am?" Encourage each one to write down short answers for how he or she thinks the following people would answer Jesus' question:

Ask: How would your mom answer Jesus' question? your teacher at school? your coach or other instructor? your best friend?

Note: You could stop at this point for this session. If they feel comfortable with the idea, encourage the tweens to ask some of the people listed above, "What do you believe about who Jesus is?" Let them bring back some of the answers to the next session. (Tell them all answers brought back to the class will be anonymous—only what people said will be reported.) You would then do the rest of this activity after they report back.

Explain that Jesus promised to build his church on the faith of Peter's confession that Jesus is "the Messiah, the Son of the living God." Encourage them to choose a few of the Scriptures below and then write their own answer to Jesus' question, "Who do you say that I am?"

Micah 5:2-5	Matthew 1:18-23	Matthew 2:1-12
Matthew 3:13-17	Matthew 17:1-8	Luke 1:26-35
Luke 1:68-69	Luke 2:1-7	Luke 2:8-20
Luke 2:41-52	Luke 4:18-19	Luke 4:38-40
Luke 4:42-43	Luke 6:17-19	

If you think your class is a little more mature and ready to push this further (many younger tween classes will not be ready, but some will), bring the class back together and let them make a class list of the things they believe about Jesus. Then have them choose from this list and write a class creed on a large sheet of paper or posterboard. Keep this creed posted in your worship area and use it for worship throughout the coming weeks.

Cumulative Cross

You will need: posterboard, colorful markers, sample of cumulative cross (see page 43).

Use symbols as a way to combine Bible study and worship during the Lenten/Easter season. A cumulative cross activity will enable you to look at the events of Holy Week and Easter. A cumulative cross is one that accumulates in sections. Each week your tweens will prepare a portion of the cross. The cumulative cross shown on page 43 was designed to be hung in the class worship area. They could make individual or group crosses.

Take a large piece of posterboard and have the tweens draw a cross. Space is needed for a circle in the middle of the cross as shown on page 43. You may use the regular cross design or a Maltese cross as shown in the example. Have them draw lines to divide the posterboard into sections.

The circle is the first piece of art for your tweens to create. The cross in the sample is based on a five-session study, including Easter. If you wish to do a six-week Lenten study, simply put the crown and nails together in one section and the bread and cup together in another section and then add two more symbols for the other sections (like the rooster for Peter's denial of Jesus and the moneybag and coins for Judas' betrayal).

Session One—Use one of the stories that tell us something about Jesus. (The loaves and fishes are used here—John 6:1-14.) Have the tweens read the story and illustrate the middle section. Let them decide which symbols should be used, then let them illustrate the symbols on the center circle.

Session Two—Palm Sunday. (It's okay to study Palm Sunday early; tweens can handle doing things this way, and they need to study the entire Holy Week story.) Have the class read Mark 11:1-10. Encourage them to illustrate the bottom section of the cross. Palm branches are used in the example.

Session Three—The Last Supper. Use Matthew 26:26-30. Divide the cross bars into two sections on each side. On the sides closest to the circle, encourage the tweens to illustrate the story. The cup and the bread are used in the example.

Session Four—Good Friday. Use any of the crucifixion stories: Matthew 27:33-56; Mark 15:22-41; Luke 23:33-49; John 19:17-37. On the outside sections of the crossbar encourage the tweens to choose symbols of the death of Jesus. The crown of thorns and the nails are used in the example.

Section Five—Easter; He is Risen! Life triumphs over death. Use any of the Resurrection stories: Matthew 28:1-10; Mark 16:1-8; Luke 24:1-12; John 20:1-10. Encourage them to choose a Resurrection symbol for the top of the cross. The butterfly is used in the example.

43

New Life Poster

You will need: Bibles, posterboard or large sheet of paper, markers.

The Bible passages below may help your tweens better understand what it means to live a new life in Jesus Christ.

Divide the class into pairs or groups and assign each pair or group one of the following passages of Scripture:
> Matthew 5:1-12
> Matthew 5:13-16
> Romans 12:9-21
> 2 Corinthians 13:4-5
> Philippians 4:10-13

Each pair or group should read their passage and think about this question: What does this passage say about new life in Christ?

Ask each pair or group to create a poster based on their Scripture passage. The poster should represent what they have learned about new life in Jesus Christ. Give each pair or group the opportunity to explain their idea of the text by sharing their new life poster. Posters should be hung in the worship area.

Note: The two passages from Matthew can be very difficult to understand. Be prepared to help the groups working on these passages. For the group that has the Beatitudes (Matthew 5:1-12), you might explain that these are statements about future rewards; that God has a different set of values than those we most often see in the world. For those who have the passage on salt and light (Matthew 5:13-16), explain that this passage tells us that because we have new life in Jesus Christ we can live a new way, we can be disciples and live so that the rest of the world sees God in us. This passage doesn't tell us to work harder, but to believe that we are the light of the world and the salt of the earth because of what God has done through Jesus.

What the pair or group see in the Bible passage should not be critiqued. Remember we all come from different understandings and different places in our spiritual growth. Further exploration of faith could be cut short by insisting upon a "correct" interpretation of the Scripture.

Together Poster

You will need: Bible; posterboard; markers; other craft items such as buttons, ribbon, and lace. Optional: magazines, scissors.

Tell your tweens that they will make a poster of the Golden Rule to hang in the worship area. In order to do this they will have to work together. As they work together, they will want to remember the Golden Rule and treat each other as they would want to be treated.

Divide up the following tasks among the members of the class. If you have a small class, you can join in this activity also. If you have a really large class, make two posters, but remember, the point is to make working together difficult and frustrating so they will have to practice the Golden Rule.

1. Have one person look up the Golden Rule in the Bible (Matthew 7:12). This person will read the Bible verse to person 2.
2. Person 2 will write the words onto the posterboard as they are read to him or her.
3. Person 3 (or more than one tween, depending upon the size of your class) should start coloring the words with different colors of markers as soon as possible.
4. Person 4 (or more than one tween, depending upon class size) can spend time deciding on what else to put on the poster and then decorate it—by drawing decorations on it, gluing pictures from magazines to it, or gluing other decorative items such as buttons, ribbon, and lace to it.
5. Any tweens who are left over can look for a good place in the classroom or hallway (near your class) to display the poster, and then be responsible for hanging up the poster when it is finished.

Before hanging the poster on the wall, have all of the tweens sign it.

The point of this activity is the interaction among the tweens. Working in crowded quarters at differing speeds can produce friction. If at any time in the process a tween starts treating another with something less than respect, have the whole group stop and repeat the Bible verse together.

The Bible on Your Own

Reading Scripture

Reading Scripture for yourself is an important way to listen for and discover the guidance of the Holy Spirit in your own life. It can also be a challenge since the Bible is full of unfamiliar words, names, places, and customs. Below are some helpful strategies for reading the Bible.

1. Ask someone you respect for help with the parts of the Bible you don't understand.

2. Follow a guide that recommends specific readings each week. This beats trying to read the Bible straight through from start to finish and getting bogged down in the Book of Leviticus. Some guides follow the seasons of the church year, so you'll read stories of Jesus' birth at Christmas and stories of Jesus' resurrection at Easter.

3. Read a passage silently, then again out loud. (Yes, even if you're the only one who is listening.) The words of Scripture were meant to be heard. Reading aloud often fills in gaps in your understanding.

4. Imagine how the people in the story are feeling. Imagine how you'd feel if you were in their shoes.

5. Ask yourself how the story connects with experiences, stories, feelings, and attitudes in your life. For example, when have you recognized you messed up badly and needed to set things straight, like Zacchaeus did?

6. Be patient. Trust the Spirit.

Advent Scripture Calendar

You will need: posterboard or large sheets of paper, photocopy of list of Scriptures, markers, craft materials.

To encourage personal use of the Bible, have your tweens make their own Advent Scripture Calendar and encourage them to use it each day, reading the Bible verse indicated, during Advent.

Give each tween a large piece of paper or posterboard. Have them draw a grid for every day of Advent (twenty-eight days). Photocopy the list of Scriptures below so that it can be posted where everyone can see it. Have them write the Scripture references on their calendar—they may arrange them in any order they wish.

Have them decorate their calendars. Challenge them to read the Scripture on the day it is listed. If your class needs motivation, make it into a contest and keep a large calendar in the classroom where they write their names on the days they actually read the Scripture.

CUT ALONG DOTTED LINE

- -

1. Psalm 25:4-5
2. Ephesians 6:13-17
3. 1 Timothy 6:11
4. Micah 6:8
5. 1 Corinthians 13:4
6. Romans 12:16
7. 1 John 4:20
8. Luke 6:31
9. 1 Timothy 6:11
10. Ephesians 6:10
11. Matthew 5:14-16
12. Matthew 11:28-30
13. Matthew 6:34
14. Romans 12:18

15. Isaiah 11:13
16. Isaiah 40:31
17. John 1:1-5
18. Luke 1:26-33
19. Luke 1:46-69
20. Matthew 1:18-21
21. Luke 2:1-7
22. Luke 2:8-14
23. Luke 2:15-20
24. Matthew 2:1-5
25. Matthew 2:7-12
26. Matthew 2:13-15
27. Matthew 2:19-21
28. John 3:16

Road Signs

Lost your direction? Use these road signs for good decision-making.

Stop: Consult the Bible before proceeding. Christians rely first on God's Word for direction. (Read Psalm 119:11.)

Go: Go with your "gut" feeling. What does your experience of the situation tell you? (Read 2 Corinthians 10:7.)

Yield: Consult the teachings of your church. The leaders and the teachings of your church can help you. (Read Proverbs 19:20.)

Caution: Think about it, using the brain God gave you. Spend some time thinking about all three of the previous things. Go to God in prayer. (Read Proverbs 13:15.)

Journaling

Introduce Your Tweens to Journaling

For some people journaling is tiresome and boring. For other people journaling becomes one of the richest forms of spiritual discipline, lasting a lifetime and providing a record of changes and growth in their personal spiritual journey.

Try introducing your tweens to this rich experience. Open their eyes to the positive aspects of journaling. For one quarter of the year, encourage them to spend five minutes in class journaling. Then let them go at it on their own, with a little guidance from you. Each week at the end of class worship time suggest a question related to what they have studied that day for the tweens to use in journaling at home. (Even if tweens say they don't like journaling, go ahead and practice it for a quarter and then continue to give a question—most journaling is done in secret.) Perhaps you will reach only one tween this way, but for that one tween you will have made a world of difference.

For the first journaling session tell your tweens that recording how we think and feel is a good spiritual discipline. It helps us pray and think about our relationship with God and others. It helps us to look back later to see how far we have progressed.

Remind them that no one will ever read their journal unless they themselves wish to let someone read it. What they write is between each individual and God. (For those who prefer art, suggest that they draw their feelings instead of writing them.)

Some possible journaling suggestions for you to give to your class of tweens:

• Where do you find God? Look for God in everything you do this week. Each day this week write down one place you find God.

• Try for one week to follow the Golden Rule. Write in your journal every time you do NOT follow the Golden Rule this week. This is a very hard rule to follow all of the time. Make a note of an especially hard time this week when you managed to keep the Golden Rule anyway.

• Yes and no—During the next week each evening think about the times you have had to say "yes" or "no" to something (even really, really small things). Write in your journal what these decisions were and whether you said "yes" or "no" (or whether you did what was asked or not). On Saturday look at the decisions from the week and decide which decisions were the most important ones. Highlight those with a marker.

- Take a look in the mirror. God made you in God's image. Look at yourself carefully. To be made in God's image does not mean that you look like God. It means that in the most important ways you are like God.

  In what ways do people see what God is like when they are with you? Each day this week think of one thing you want people to know about God and try to think how you can be that way that day.

  For example: God is loving. On Monday, concentrate on being loving all day—even to the school bully and to your younger brother. God brings joy. On Tuesday, concentrate on trying to approach everything (even school) with a joyful attitude.

  Record your ups and downs and your feelings about them in your journal. (By the way, trying to be a reflection of God doesn't mean you are perfect as God is perfect. You will make mistakes. Remember God is forgiving, and God forgives you if you repent and honestly try again.)

- Christian at school—In America it's pretty easy to say we are Christians. In most places people accept that. But each of us needs to try to live up to the name *Christian* and make it a name of which to be proud. Think about this and write the answer to the following question in your journal: What does it mean to be Christian at school? List some ways that Christians should treat their fellow tweens. Are there some activities that Christians shouldn't participate in? Are there activities that Christians should gladly participate in?

- Christian discipleship—God calls all people—even tweens—to be faithful disciples. What are your feelings about God calling someone your age to be a faithful disciple? What does being a disciple mean to you?

- Priority list—In your journal list the top ten priorities in your life. Then rearrange them in order of importance—which is first, which is second, and so forth. Where does God fit in the list? Is going to church on the list at all?

- Temptation challenge—Are you strong enough to beat temptation? Try these challenges and see:
    1. Fast for an hour from television, junk food, video games, or your favorite activity. Use your journal to focus on God.
    2. Do you test God by asking for unreasonable things? Try asking God for greater faith.
    3. Think of one way you can serve God this week by serving others.
    4. Try to spend one whole day at school without making fun of anyone. Say only nice things. (It's harder than you think.)

    RATE YOURSELF: The greatest challenge of all is to rate yourself and be completely honest. In your journal draw a scale from 1 to 10, where 10 is the best score on the scale. Rate yourself on the challenges on your scale.

Creeds and Covenants

A creed can be used as a tool to help your tweens think about what they believe. A covenant helps them come to an understanding of the importance of committing to something.

Write a Class Creed

You will need: large sheets of paper, markers.

Explain that a creed is a statement that tells what someone believes. Use two large sheets of paper. Write at the top of one sheet of paper, "We believe God is…" Write in the middle of the sheet of paper, "We believe Jesus is…" Write further down the sheet of paper, "We believe the church is…" Post this paper where the tweens can see it.

Ask your tweens to brainstorm things they believe about God, Jesus, and the church. Write their ideas under the appropriate headings on the paper.

Encourage the tweens to discuss and agree upon which ideas from their brainstorming list they want to keep in their creed. Write the finished creed on the second sheet of paper. Have the tweens read the creed together.

Give your pastor a copy of the creed. Suggest that the creed be printed in your church bulletin and used in your worship service. You might also suggest that your class participate in the worship service and lead the congregation in reciting the creed.

What Do You Believe?

You will need: large sheets of paper, markers.

Have the tweens name ten things they believe in and list these on a large sheet of paper. (They do not all have to be religious, but they need to be things that seem to be unable to be proved. Tweens might say almost anything. Be sure that of the ten listed, at least one is a religious belief.)

Choose one of the religious beliefs they named and together discuss this belief. This will probably be difficult even for you, but it is a very good exercise in having your tweens begin to think theologically for themselves. You may have incomplete answers; that is okay.

At the next session revisit your list and have the class add one more religious belief to the list. Repeat this each week, adding one more religious belief per week. At the end of this quarter write out all the statements regarding religious beliefs onto one large sheet of paper. You now have a creed of the class' main beliefs.

Extraordinary Covenant

Anyone working with young adolescents knows that they can be a handful at times. Rather than scaling back your expectations to match behaviors, consider raising those expectations a bit. Young persons will often respond to the suggestion that they are capable of tackling greater challenges.

Explain that a covenant is unique (different from a contract or even a promise) in that it starts by acknowledging what God has already done for us, and then it invites us to respond. Reminding them that God has done and continues to do extraordinary things through ordinary people like Joseph and Mary, ask them to come up with no more than five extraordinary things they can agree or covenant together to do for the Advent season. These might be related to Sunday school classroom behaviors, opportunities to reach out to persons in the community, or things that they might do at home to prepare for Christmas or to help make others' preparations more manageable.

A covenant of this type could also be adapted for use during the Lenten/Easter season.

Make a Class Covenant

Tell your tweens that we all need agreements to live by or we become confused, have fights, or just don't know what to do. Create a class covenant specifying how class members will treat one another and how the class will deal with problems in a positive manner.

Let the class as a group come up with three ways to deal positively with class conflict. Guide them only if they get silly, too judgmental, or unable to think of anything. You must be sure that the final agreement is one that you can live with also. Do not be too surprised if they are harder on one another than you might be on them. After agreement is reached on the three rules, have each tween sign the covenant. Every class member must sign the covenant, including you. Post the covenant in a prominent spot in the room for the rest of the quarter; read it to the class if a situation arises where they need to be reminded of the covenant to which they all agreed.

Year of Peace Commitment

When studying violence in any of its forms, you might want to encourage your tweens to adopt a covenant such as the one below that commits everyone to act peacefully for a full year. The covenant should be signed by all, posted in a prominent place, and referred to frequently.

Your tweens might even want to involve the rest of the church in this commitment. They could encourage the congregation to join them in this effort by writing articles for the church newsletter, making announcements in church services, and creating and performing skits for the congregation that show nonviolent solutions to problems. You might even bring a counselor in to help teach them how problems are solved nonviolently before creating the skits.

CUT ALONG DOTTED LINE

Year of Peace Commitment Card

In this church and in this life:

1. There will be no violence against any persons; no physical or verbal abuse based on race, creed, gender, or sexual orientation.
2. I will demonstrate respect for everyone, and accept his or her concerns, encouraging anyone who provides a role model for his or her peers.
3. There will be protection and consolation for victims of violence.
4. I will oppose the use and glorification of violence in the media and in our culture.
5. There will be a commitment to nonviolent resolution of conflict.
6. I will practice respect and love for the earth and all of God's creation.

By signing this commitment to peace, I pledge to support nonviolence in this church and in our community by examining my own actions, and to make every effort to practice nonviolence in my life.

Signed,

_____

Disciple Commitment Card

You will need: photocopies of Disciple Commitment Card (below), envelopes.

Talk with your tweens about true discipleship, which means more than just saying we are good disciples. Good discipleship requires commitment and the discipline to follow through with commitments.

Ask: What is a commitment? *(a pledge or a promise to do something)*

Tweens are now old enough to make a real commitment to be followers of Jesus. Disciples of Jesus regularly study the Scriptures, pray, worship, and do acts of ministry.

Make photocopies of the Disciple Commitment Card below, one for each tween.

Ask your tweens as disciples to think about how they will commit to serving Jesus over the next month. Encourage them to take a Disciple Commitment Card and write on it their personal commitment. Assure them that no one else will read their card. When they have finished, have them sign the card. Have them put the card in an envelope and address is to themselves. Tell them that you will mail the Disciple Commitment Card to them as a reminder of what they have pledged to do for the next month.

CUT ALONG DOTTED LINE

Disciple Commitment Card

As a disciple of Jesus Christ I commit for the next month to:

Pray for:

Help others by:

Attend worship and Sunday school these Sundays:

Read my Bible_____ minutes a day.

Signed,

_____

Service

Spirituality is about our whole being, our whole lives. One of the greatest ways for tweens to grow spiritually is through service and outreach. Tweens naturally love doing service, especially if they can interact with the people they are serving, and nothing connects spirituality to life like serving real people in a real way.

Ministry Inventory

You will need: large sheet of paper or dry erase board, markers.

Every Christian is blessed with a variety of gifts to use for ministry in the church. Before you start a service project, complete a ministry inventory with your group to discover their gifts and their interests.

Write out the list below on a large sheet of paper or a dry erase board and ask your tweens to write their names under those things that they are good at and like to do. Add anything to the list that is appropriate for your group and area. As a group think of the different areas in your church and community where you can use your gifts. Use this list for helping to decide in what service projects your group can participate.

Gifts and Interest List

- art: drawing
- art: painting
- art: other _____
- cleaning and organizing cabinets
- cooking/baking
- greeter: Sunday morning worship
- greeter: Sunday school class
- helping with activities for younger children
- helping in the office
- computers
- library work
- lighting the altar candles/acolyte
- mowing lawns
- music: singing
- music: playing an instrument
- photography
- praying for others
- reading Scripture in the worship service
- recycling
- talking on the phone
- ushering
- writing

Pass on the Faith

Lead your tweens in passing on their faith to a younger children's class in the church. Help your tweens find ways to get to know the children. Take them to the class during Sunday school at a time prearranged with the teacher of the younger class, and have your tweens choose a child and tell that child some of the stories they know from the Bible. Or have your class of tweens turn a Bible story into a drama and perform it for the younger class.

Ask the teacher of the younger class to approve times when your tween class can visit during the year and get to know the younger children. Your tween class can do this by:
• Asking the younger children questions (what's your birthday? do you have pets? what's your favorite video? and so forth).
• Teaching them something. Has your class learned to sign a Bible verse in American Sign Language? Teach the younger children to do it.
• Reading to the younger children.
• Putting on a puppet show of a Bible story.
• Making a present and a card for each younger child's birthday.

Help your tweens brainstorm additional ideas for how they can pass on their faith to the younger children's class.

Helping God's People

Here are some suggestions for service:

• Make a care package for someone who is sick.
• Bake cookies and take them to a nursing home.
• Stay after church this Sunday and pick up all the bulletins and other things left in the pews after the service.
• Make a Bible storybook for young children. Take or send it to a place where children need books but cannot afford a lot of them.
• Ask everyone in the class to make a donation from their own allowances. Use the money for disaster relief and send it to the Red Cross or an agency that your church supports.
• Sit with an older person in church and learn more about him or her.

Places to Serve

Tweens are naturally into service, but at times we all need ideas where to serve. Check with your pastor, your missions committee, local agencies, and your national church organization. Listed below are some worthy organizations.

New Churches—When a new church begins it often doesn't have enough money to pay a pastor, build a building, and buy curriculum and toys for a nursery. Find a new church in your area. Do your tweens have books and old toys (in good condition) that they can donate? Raise money to help the church purchase some Bibles for the church's Sunday school classrooms.

Missionary Support—Missionaries are a long way from home, and they need help to do their work. Often they work in countries that have very little. But one of the biggest ways to help support missionaries is through letters! They enjoy getting letters from their home country, and the missionaries can help educate your tweens as to the people and conditions in the country they are serving. Pick a missionary and let your group become pen pals with a missionary.

America's Second Harvest—This national network of more than two hundred food banks distributes donated food to hungry Americans. Have a food collection drive and then as a group take the canned food and help sort for an afternoon. Your help will be appreciated. You will need to make an appointment with the food bank for the time you are to take the food and to sort it. This is a project tweens really get into because they can actively participate in it.

Heifer International—An international organization attempting to end hunger around the world by helping grass-roots community groups who determine their own needs. They distribute livestock, helping people grow their own herds and become responsible for their own livelihood. Your group may want to raise money for a chicken, a goat, or a cow. Check it out on the internet at www.heifer.org.

Bethlehem Centers, Salvation Army, Goodwill Industries—These organizations all collect donations of old items to help those who are less fortunate. Recycle some of those old clothes and toys in your tweens' closets. As a class have a drive and see how much just your tweens can bring. Then you might want to expand this activity to the whole church. Let your tween class be the sponsor, do the advertising, and put collection containers around the church.

With any of the above service projects, spend some time helping your tweens learn more about the organization you are going to help. For local organizations, plan a group visit, and/or bring someone in from the organization to speak to your class. Often with national organizations there will be a branch in your city or a location nearby. Invite someone in, or ask them to send you more information. Search the internet for more information; just be sure that you find a legitimate organization and not a group using a variation of the name of a legitimate organization. Connect all service projects to Bible study and worship time.

CAUTION: Never visit a web site unless you know it's a good site. Also, remember that web addresses can often change.

Be a Servant

The story of Jesus washing the feet of the disciples in John 13:1-20 demonstrates the perfect example of servanthood. Reading this story or other stories of servanthood provide a time for practicing servanthood.

The following is a list of some ways for your tweens to practice servanthood.

Servant to Your Community—Lead a brainstorming session about things that need to be done in your community; or ask your tweens to find out what opportunities for service are available from the newspaper, the internet, or by talking to people. Some possibilities are raking leaves for the elderly, cleaning up a section of a public park, or washing windows at the local school.

Servant to Your Church—Go on a "servanthood treasure hunt." Have your tweens talk with the pastor, the church secretary, the custodian (if present in the building), leaders of other classes, and so forth, and discover what are some of the things that need to be done around the church.

Bring the group back together and have them use the "treasure" of ideas they have gathered to decide upon one area in which to be a "servant group" this month. Some possible projects include cleaning a room, videotaping (or tape recording) a worship service for a church member who is homebound or hospitalized, helping the secretary fold bulletins for the worship service, washing toys in the nursery, and so forth.

Servant to Your Family—This is the most difficult place for a tween to be a servant. They often already feel (rightly or wrongly) like a servant in their own homes. The point is for them to be a servant from their hearts without it being asked or expected of them.

Ask the group to brainstorm ways to be a servant at home. Then challenge them to pick one way and to do it. For accountability, they are to report back to the class what they did during the week and how it was received.

Some ideas for at-home service are to set the dinner table without being asked and make it especially beautiful or interesting, make place cards with a personal note of appreciation for each member of the family, do a chore that is normally done by a sibling, sweep or vacuum the home, or feed the pets every day before being asked to do so.

Music

Music is not only a wonderful source for evoking emotional responses, but also a major source of theology.

• Praise choruses and contemporary Christian music are fun.

• Praise choruses and contemporary Christian music often use non-inclusive language and only male images of God.

• Praise choruses and contemporary Christian music are high on praise, but often are short on theology with depth.

Use praise choruses and contemporary Christian music, but include generous amounts of music that will be heard in worship also. Use hymns and songs that have a depth of theological ideas and richness. It's good to know that God is awesome, but it's more important to know why God is awesome.

Remember that the average adult has received a large amount of his or her theology from hymns.

Sing and Sign

Tweens often relate to music when signing is included. Why not engage both your musical and your physical learners by singing and signing a song using American Sign Language?

For example, if you are studying Moses, you might want to try to sing and sign "Go Down, Moses." This is a call response song. One person sings the call sections of the verse; everyone else responds with the repeated phrase, "Let my people go." As they sing the response have them sign the words also.

Go Down, Moses
When Israel was in Egypt's land,
let my people go;
oppressed so hard they could not stand,
let my people go.
Go down, Moses, way down in Egypt's land;
tell old Pharaoh to let my people go!

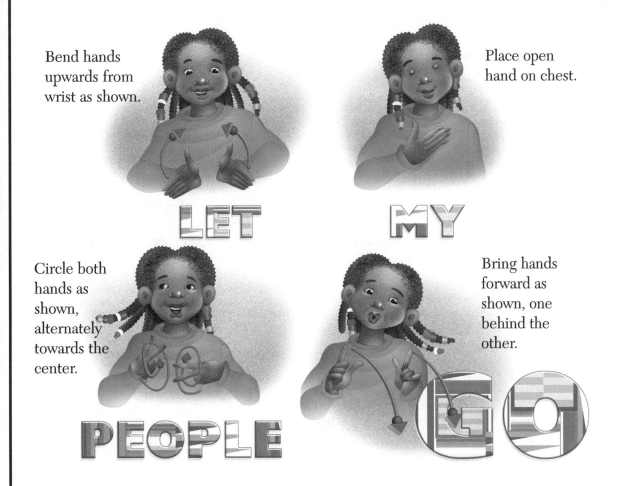

Bend hands upwards from wrist as shown.

LET

Place open hand on chest.

MY

Circle both hands as shown, alternately towards the center.

PEOPLE

Bring hands forward as shown, one behind the other.

GO

Text for "Go Down, Moses" from *The United Methodist Hymnal*,
copyright © 1989 The United Methodist Publishing House, No. 448.

Dramatize a Hymn of Discipleship

You will need: cassette/CD of your choosing.
Optional: words to the selected hymn of discipleship.

Choose a hymn or song that relates to discipleship from a cassette or CD owned by you or your church. Some possibilities are: "Here I Am, Lord," "Have Thine Own Way, Lord," "O Jesus, I Have Promised," "Take Time to Be Holy," and "Take My Life, and Let It Be."

Let the tweens listen to the music. Divide the class into groups and let each group decide how to dramatize the hymn. How would they be disciples at home? at school? on the baseball field? at a party? and so forth. Let each group present their own dramatization.

For a variation, you could have each group dramatize a different hymn of discipleship.

Note: This activity will be much easier for the groups if you provide words to the hymns for your tweens to read.

Pick a Psalm

You will need: Bibles (one for each tween).

Divide your tweens into groups of three. Make sure that every person in each group has a Bible.

Talk about how Psalms are written in poetry form and are often used in worship, either read aloud or arranged musically. Give the groups three minutes to find a psalm they would like to suggest for worship. Tell them that they will be asked to give the reason they chose that particular psalm.

After three minutes bring the groups back together to suggest their psalm. Then let the class choose which psalm they will use in the closing worship today.

Note: A variation on this would be to have each group find a psalm (or section of a psalm) that fits the particular topic you are studying today. Another variation would be to have each group present their psalm in some form: by singing if they can find it in a hymnal, by reading it, by making it into a litany, or by making it into a prayer.

Conduct a Psalm Hunt

You will need: Bibles, hymnals, paper, pencils, large sheet of paper or dry erase board, markers.

Divide your tweens into groups of three or four. Give each participant a copy of your church's hymnal or song book. Ask each group to elect a person to be the recorder. This person needs paper and a pencil.

Say: The Psalms were the worship hymns of the Hebrew people. These ancient hymns continue to be used in our modern worship—both Jewish and Christian. Also, the ancient biblical Psalms have inspired modern hymns.

Give the following instructions to the groups.

• This will be a psalm hunt—a hunt to see which group can find the most references to specific Psalms in the hymnal. (Clue: Look at the bottom of each hymn where the composer is listed; Scripture references may be listed there also.)

• The recorder for each group is to record the hymn number for later reference. Each psalm reference will be worth one point. If you know the hymn that was inspired by a psalm, and you can sing the first verse, your group will get five points for singing it. The team with the most points wins. You will have five minutes for your psalm hunt.

After five minutes, stop the hunt. Have each recorder count the number of psalm references. The group with the most references goes first. List them on a large sheet of paper or dry erase board as they are named so that all groups can check their lists against the first team's list. Every group that named those hymns gets a point. After the first group has read off their list, have any group that has one or more different hymns listed read those numbers out to you. They get points for their hymn references. Check hymn references if questions arise.

Then have groups sing the first verses of hymns they know that are inspired by Psalms to earn their extra points.

Look at Hymns

You will need: hymnals, pencils, paper, large sheet of paper or dry erase board, markers.

Divide your tweens into pairs or small groups. Be sure to have a hymnal for each participant. Ask the tweens to turn to the "Index of Topics and Categories" section found in the back of the hymnal. Then ask them to turn to the category "Justice."

Have the groups find as many hymns as they can that focus on justice.

Ask: What other category is listed that also deals with issue of justice? (for example, Social Concerns) **How many hymns are found in this category?**

Note: Not all hymnals categorize their hymns in this way. If your hymnal does not have these categories, look through the hymns themselves and find hymns with themes of justice, peace, and social concerns. Some justice hymns include "Immortal, Invisible, God Only Wise," "Hail to the Lord's Anointed," "There's a Wideness in God's Mercy," and "For the Healing of the Nations."

Then assign one hymn to each group. Be sure that each group is assigned a different hymn. They are to look at their hymn to pick out key words and phrases that talk about justice.

When they have finished bring all of the groups back together to share their findings. Ask one person to report for each group while you write the words or phrases on a large piece of paper or on an erasable board.

Let the tweens look at the phrases and then lead a discussion about the ideas and words found in the hymns. When your combined list is finished, they may find that some words or ideas are repeated.

Ask: Why do you think this happens? What does it tell us about these words or phrases?

This activity centers on hymns of justice, but it would work equally well for any number of topics—peace, love, joy, thankfulness, names for Jesus, trust in God, and discipleship.

Practice and Deliver Carolgrams

You will need: cassette/CD with Christmas music, cassette/CD player, pencil and paper or computer with printer to make forms.

Explain to the tweens that one way to help others prepare for Christmas is through Christmas caroling. Tell the tweens that they will be delivering carolgrams to the other Sunday school classes on the Sunday before Christmas. The other classes will request a carol in advance from a prepared list and your class, as a group, will visit each class and sing the requested carol.

• As a class compile a list of Christmas carols that your tweens feel comfortable singing.

• Make a photocopy of this list. Distribute it to youth and adult classes, and ask them to choose a carol on the list for your group to sing. The form should state the date you will be caroling and designate a date the forms are to be returned to your class.

• Have your tweens practice the carols they will sing. Be sure that they know the words.

• Design a plan for visiting the Sunday school classes that have requested carolgrams. It would be most efficient to visit all classes in one area of the church before moving to the other classes.

• Have the tweens tell the classes they visit that they are delivering carolgrams because they want to share the joy of Jesus' birth. Be sure to end your visit by wishing everyone a Merry Christmas.

Easter Caroling

You will need: cassette/CD and cassette/CD player, or someone from your church's Music Department and an instrument.

Have someone from the music department come in (if you don't feel qualified) and help your tweens learn some rousing Easter hymns. Remember that today's tweens don't hear hymns except in church, and that they may be unfamiliar with many of them.

Then on Easter Sunday (during the Sunday school hour) take them "Easter Caroling" to the adult Sunday school classes.

If you have time on the Saturday before Easter or the Monday night after Easter take the tweens to a nursing home or to the homes of those church members who are sick or homebound and let them go "Easter Caroling." If you use this option and you go after Easter service (or sometime during the week after Easter), the church might allow you to take the lilies that were in the sanctuary and give them as gifts to the people to whom you are singing.

Share the Good News

We all have the opportunity to share with others the good news. Encourage your tweens to share the good news in song.

Let them choose a song (any song that they like and that is easy to sing) and write Christian lyrics to the song; or write singing telegrams and sing them to other Sunday school classes.

Illustrate a Song

You will need: recording of "Let There Be Peace on Earth," cassette/CD player, paper, paints.

Tell your tweens that words can sometimes paint a picture, and that poets often seek to create an emotion-filled picture. Have the tweens close their eyes and listen as you read, sing, or play the words to the song "Let There Be Peace on Earth."

Encourage the tweens to paint a picture about the words of the song. Tell them that they may illustrate the song as they desire. They may paint images that come to mind; or, they may create pictures with colors that express the emotions evoked by the song, using no recognizable images.

The Tale the Music Tells

You will need: cassette/CD of your favorite hymn or Christian song, cassette/CD player.

Choose any Christian hymn or song that you feel is particularly meaningful or one that will be meaningful to your tweens. Ask everyone to close his or her eyes and just listen to the music. Ask them to think about the feelings that are being shared through the music.

Play the music again, and this time invite the tweens to draw a picture or write a poem, story, or song that describes the feelings being shared by the music.

Ask: How did you know that the music was sharing the feelings you described?

Create a Dance

You will need: Bibles.

Tell your tweens how liturgical dance, like signing, uses more than just our hands to communicate a message to others. As an example use Acts 10:34b-35: "I truly understand that God shows no partiality, but in every nation anyone who fears him and does what is right is acceptable to him." Together read the Bible verse and lead a discussion on what kind of movements a dance could use to tell the message of Acts 10:34b-35.

Ask: What words in that verse make you think of a gesture or movement? How could you move to show that word when it is read?

Ask: Which words have similar meanings to *partiality* and *acceptable*? Will different words change how the movements are performed?

Allow for exploration and experimentation. Ask your pastor if your tweens may perform the movements for the congregation during worship.

This activity could be used with a large number of Bible verses.

Write a Song

You will need: pencil, paper, large sheet of paper, marker.

Have the tweens work as a class to write a song about a conflict they have had. Encourage the tweens to include ideas from conflict resolution and the Golden Rule in their song ending; or, they might wish to write a song about the Golden Rule itself. Suggest that they might want to use a familiar tune, or they can make up a tune themselves.

Sing the song now; or, if you wish, make plans to sing it during a worship service.

If your class wishes to present the song in a worship service, be sure to get permission in advance. Also, give the class at least three weeks to practice the song before presenting it.

Sing, Dance, Enjoy

You will need: recording of "Lord of the Dance," cassette/CD player.

Get a recording of the song "Lord of the Dance" (or ask your church musician if someone in the church can make a recording of the hymn for you).

Play the song for your tweens. Have the words on hand (they are in some hymnals) and encourage them to sing along.

This song just begs people to dance to it. Encourage your tweens to get up and dance around the room. One great way to do this is to have them do a line dance. Choose a leader and let him or her do movements—whatever feels right to him or her. (Perhaps for the first leader pick someone you know has some dancing experience.) The others are to imitate the movements of that leader. Have a different leader for each verse of the dance.

It is also okay to be much less formal with this song and to just let each tween dance to the music in any way he or she chooses.

Other Church Settings

In learning settings other than Sunday school, there is often more time to offer in-depth spiritual opportunities and/or experiences outside of the church building.

Other Church Settings

Take advantage of other church settings (such as after-school programs, Sunday evening fellowships, Wednesday night programs, retreats, and so forth) to do some unique activities related to tween spirituality.

• Do a short-term study on prayer—a full month to six weeks. Or, spend one whole night concentrating on the Lord's Prayer (see pages 75-80).

• Plan for a longer worship time—10 to 15 minutes.

• Do special event worship times. Let the tweens prepare a short worship as part of a special event night and invite the parents.

• Is there a prayer labyrinth anywhere near you? Take your tweens and let them walk the labyrinth (see page 72).

• Teach your tweens the origin and meaning of Christian symbols. Tweens are really beginning to comprehend the full significance of symbols—take them deeper into this area (and have fun at the same time).

• Use American Sign Language as part of the event. Tweens love the action of signing, and it makes the experience of learning the Bible verse more memorable.

• Teach the "language of faith." Everyone needs a way to talk about his or her faith and to share his or her beliefs. Without the "language," it is easy for misunderstandings or frustrations to occur.

• Use creeds. These collective statements of faith provide a lasting foundation. Familiarity with creeds now will breed comfort in the future.

• Do missions together. Working side-by-side to reach out to others does good for the spirit within each of us that is impossible to duplicate any other way.

• Provide opportunities for tweens to lead their own worship experiences. However, do not leave them stranded. Most tweens are not prepared to lead worship on their own. Provide specific ways they can lead worship, and give them all the worship resources at hand. Given the opportunity and the proper tools, worship can become a moment they anticipate (see pages 91-94 for some helps).

Activities

Field Trips

You will need: signed copy of permission slip for each tween (see page 123), transportation, adult chaperones.

Many denominations own and operate hospitals, retirement centers, children's homes, and other institutions that provide care for those who have special needs. Plan to visit such an institution if one is located nearby.

Before taking the field trip:

• help your tweens think about what they are going to see and why such places exist.

• advise the tweens about any rules or restrictions that apply to their visit.

• arrange transportation.

• get a signed permission slip for each tween attending the field trip from his or her parents or guardians. (A sample permission slip is on page 123. Please feel free to copy and use it.)

• give tweens any written information that they might need.

After the trip, encourage the tweens to talk about their experiences. Follow the field trip with a shared activity, such as making and sending greeting cards, making tray favors, or writing an article for the church newsletter telling about what was learned on the field trip.

Some other types of field trips are experiencing or learning field trips (see pages 72 and 73 for two suggestions for this type of field trip).

Field Trip: Walk a Labyrinth

You will need: signed copy of permission slip for each tween (see page 123), transportation, adult chaperones.

In a few areas of the United States there are now full-sized prayer labyrinths that can be walked. Look for one near you, and take a field trip to this location with your tweens. Before you go provide them with information about a prayer labyrinth.

Say: The labyrinth is a spiritual tool that many people use to grow closer to God. When you walk the labyrinth, you have to be careful to stay on the correct path, so you concentrate on your feet. As you walk, you are asked to be quiet and to listen for God's Word. When you reach the center of the labyrinth, you are to sit down and remain as long as you like, meditating on God. Then, you walk out as you came in, still in silence, still listening for God. The labyrinth is designed to lead you closer to God, much like a shepherd leads the sheep. Through spiritual tools such as prayer, Bible reading, and worship, we know that we are children of God.

Be prepared for your tweens to be glad of the field trip, but indifferent to the labyrinth. However, you might be surprised at their response when they have finished the labyrinth walk.

If you do not have a labyrinth nearby, photocopy and use the finger labyrinth below for worship. Give them the following instructions:

Say: Look at the labyrinth and use your finger and follow the path as you pray for family, friends, and any other concerns you may have.

Field Trip: Other Styles of Worship

Talk with your tweens about the centrality of worship in the Bible and in the lives of Christians today.

Have them explore some Scriptures pertaining to worship (perhaps dividing into groups to discover what the Bible says and reporting back to the entire group). The following are some of the biblical references relating to worship:

Exodus 8:1
1 Chronicles 16:29
Psalm 100:2
Psalm 132:7
Jonah 1:9
Zechariah 14:16
Matthew 4:10
John 4:23
Acts 8:27

Encourage your tweens to tell about different styles of worship they have observed by visiting other churches, by attending camp, or by watching a movie or television program.

Go on a field trip to another church in your community that has a style of worship different than yours. This may be a church of another denomination—Protestant, Catholic, or Eastern Orthodox. It may be a church of your own denomination that worships in a completely different style than your church does.

Make arrangements with the minister, pastor, or priest before you go to have someone meet you before the worship service to explain anything you may need to know (in what parts of the service you may participate, how you will know when to sit or stand, and so forth).

When you return discuss with your tweens what they saw and heard, how they felt, what if anything made them feel uncomfortable, and what was different about the style of worship. Let them dig a little deeper by discussing what if any differences they feel are really important.

Town Meeting in Antioch

You will need: Bibles, photocopy of background information for each group.
Optional: gavel for "mayor."

This town meeting is based on a study of Acts 11:19-26, when the name "Christian" was first applied to the followers of Jesus.

> **Say: There is speculation that the name "Christians" was first used as a derogatory word. It was used to make fun of these people who did things in strange ways. The city of Antioch was not always happy about everything these "Christians" did. After all, the Christians didn't worship the local idols. They made general nuisances of themselves. A town meeting has been called to decide what to do.**

Divide the class into three groups: followers of Jesus, city council members, and angry townspeople. Ask the groups to choose spokespeople. Make a photocopy of the small block of background information below to give to the different groups participating in the town meeting so that they can prepare.

As the groups are preparing, go to the angry townspeople and quietly give them the instructions that they should murmur when they agree or disagree with someone, and that sometimes they should shout "Christians" in a taunting voice to those in the other group when they are speaking.

Then quietly go to the followers of Jesus and tell them that they may murmur among themselves and when they speak, they may speak passionately, but that as followers of Jesus they should always treat the other side with respect, no matter what happens. They should never interrupt nor should they get angry at the townspeople, even when the townspeople are rude and obnoxious.

After the groups have had a few minutes to prepare, bring them together for the town meeting. Have the city council members sit at a table with the town council chairperson in the middle. The other two groups should mingle together and sit in chairs facing the council. In order to speak, a person must rise and stand in front of the table.

The council chairperson will conduct the meeting and ask different sides to speak. If things get out of hand, the mayor should bang the gavel and ask for order. Limit the time for the meeting according to your session time.

CUT ALONG DOTTED LINE ⬊

- -

Background Information

Some of the things Christians are doing:

- Preaching in the streets.
- Living together in groups.
- Providing meals for the poor in a residential area. (Therefore, there are many poor people moving to the area, which some townspeople feel causes more crime and costs too much money.)
- Asking people to change from their old ways of doing things and to act differently (this causes social unrest).
- Telling people they should be worshiping only one God instead of worshiping the latest "god."

Lord's Prayer Event

Choose one or all of the following activities to do a major event for your
tweens that is centered around digging deeper into the Lord's Prayer (Matthew 6:9-13).

Envision the Lord's Prayer

You will need: six large sheets of paper, markers, tape to post mural.

Invite your tweens to create a six-part mural, each part illustrating a portion of the Lord's
Prayer. Write a portion of the Lord's Prayer on each of six large sheets of paper, or on six
separate sections of a long sheet of mural paper. Give the tweens colored markers and have
them put on paper the mental pictures that come to their minds as they hear the various
portions of the prayer.

Write a Prayer

You will need: pencil and paper for each tween, large posterboard, markers.

Encourage your tweens to brainstorm different ways that they use prayer. If they have difficulty
expressing how they pray, have them name different times when they pray, such as mealtime,
morning, before going to bed, when people are sick or in trouble, and so forth.

When the brainstorming session is finished, remind the tweens that when the disciples asked
Jesus how to pray he gave them an example, the Lord's Prayer.

Have the tweens write their own prayers using the Lord's Prayer as a model. Do this by
displaying a large posterboard with the Lord's Prayer divided into sections. (The following
example uses the Lord's Prayer found in Matthew 6:9-13 from the NRSV translation of the
Bible. For this activity, use whatever version of the Lord's Prayer is traditionally used by your
church.) For example, the first verse says, "Our Father in heaven, hallowed be your name."
Suggest that this describes our relationship with God. The second verse puts God in charge of
the whole world. The third verse asks for the things that are necessary for us to live. The fourth
verse asks for forgiveness, and reminds us of the Golden Rule ("in everything do to others as
you would have them do to you" Matthew 7:12). The verse, "And do not bring us to the time of
trial, but rescue us from the evil one," is asking for God's help in our resisting evil and sin. The
last part of the prayer is called the hymn of praise. The portion of the prayer called the hymn
of praise is a traditional addition to the prayer used by Protestants.

Encourage your tweens to put their own concerns into these types of sentences.

Move in Prayer

You will need: photocopy of "The Lord's Prayer in Motion" (see pages 79-80).

Make an enlarged photocopy of "The Lord's Prayer in Motion" (pages 79-80). Post these pages where they can be seen. Invite your tweens to work together to move through each phrase. If you have a large class, display the poster in a central location and assign each group a section of the prayer.

Groups and individuals should refer to the poster and work together to determine how best to incorporate motions to the words of the prayer. Then have them come together and teach each other to pray using the body motions.

Create Interpretive Movement

You will need: cassette/CD player, cassette/CD recording of "The Lord's Prayer."

Work with one of the many different recordings of "The Lord's Prayer" (your church may have one on hand) and help the tweens create movement (not signing, but whole body movement) that expresses the words and the feelings of the Lord's Prayer. Approach the pastor or another worship leader or planner about using this in worship some Sunday in the near future.

Make a Lord's Prayer Bracelet

You will need (for each tween): four pieces of heavy string or cord—a pair of two-foot pieces and a pair of four-foot pieces, ten glow-in-the-dark beads.

Have a Lord's Prayer bracelet prepared ahead of time as a model, and be comfortable with the process so you can demonstrate how it is done.

1. Put the ends of the four pieces of heavy string or cord together, side by side, shorter strings in the center.
2. Place a piece of tape across the pieces of string, six inches from the ends, and fasten the string securely to the edge of a table with the tape.
3. Wrap a one-inch piece of tape around the short center pieces, like the end of a shoelace.
4. Bring the right long string over the center strings and under the left long string, leaving a loop in the right long string. Loop the left long string under the right long string, under the center strings, and up and all the way through the loop on the right. Pull the knot tight, up to the tape. You've just done a half-knot.
5. Repeat the same process, but in reverse. Left side over the centers, leaving a loop on the left, under the right side. Right side under the left, under the centers, up and all the way through the loop. Pull the knot tight. You have a square knot.
6. Repeat Steps 4 and 5 two more times to create three square knots.
7. Slide your first bead over the taped end of the center strings and up to the knots.
8. Repeat Step 4 six times to create a spiral. Don't try to prevent the center strings from rotating. Simply adjust the position of your hands as you tie. Add another bead.
9. Continue tying six half knots and adding a bead until all ten beads have been placed on the center strings.
10. After the tenth bead is added, repeat Steps 4, 5, and 6.
11. Bring the end square knots together. Gather the four center strings together with two of the long strings on the right, and two on the left. Treat the strings on the right as one string, likewise the strings on the left. Tie three more square knots.
12. Trim off the ends, put the bracelet on your wrist, and pray the Lord's Prayer as you slide your other hand from bead to bead, saying a portion of the prayer as you pause at each bead, such as

    1. Our Father, who art in heaven,
    2. hallowed be thy name.
    3. Thy kingdom come,
        and so forth

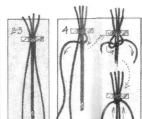

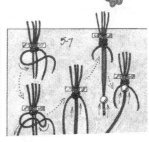

Lord's Prayer Meditation

You will need: Bible.

Ask the tweens to get into a position where they can remain comfortable for several minutes without having to shift around. When they have done so, ask them to take a deep breath, hold it for a few seconds, and then release it slowly. Repeat two more times. The last time, ask them to imagine that all of the stress in their bodies is draining away as they slowly release their breath. Ask them to close their eyes, and to quietly listen to and think about what you will be saying.

Read Luke 11:1. **Say: Luke 11:1 tells us that Jesus had been praying "in a certain place" when he taught his disciples the Lord's Prayer. The verse doesn't tell us what that certain place was, but it implies that there was a special place where Jesus liked to go for prayer with his disciples. In your imagination, let yourself wander off to a place that you envision as a place of prayer. While this will be your private place, let a part of your mind remain aware of the others with you in this place. All prayer is corporate prayer. Corporate prayer is a prayer offered by more than one person. When we go to God in prayer, we are joined by the people who have taught us to pray, the people who have been our prayer models, as well as the people for whom we are praying.**

Imagine yourself inviting Jesus to join you in your special place. Watch him as he bows his head and prays. When he is done, hear yourself asking, "Lord, teach us to pray." As you listen to his response—to how the church prays it today—be aware of the images that come to your mind and the feelings that come to your body.

As you repeat the prayer, do so slowly, as follows, allowing time for your tweens to form their images.

Say: "When you pray, say: Our Father, who art in heaven, hallowed be thy name." Heavenly Parent, your name is holy, your name is unlike any other, because you are unlike all others. (Pause) **"Thy kingdom come, thy will be done on earth as it is in heaven." O God, let your desires, your will become the will and the desire of all people, that we might see your realm established on earth as you have established it in heaven.** (Pause) **"Give us this day our daily bread." O God, you know the needs of all the earth. We ask that you would meet today's needs, not tomorrow's, but just today's. Our greatest need is for you, so we do not ask for too much all at once. Give us enough for today, and we will come tomorrow and ask you for tomorrow's bread.** (Pause) **"And forgive us our trespasses, as we forgive those who trespass against us." No sin is greater than your ability to forgive. Let us be as ready to forgive those whose sins have touched us and hurt us, as we are to receive your forgiveness for our own thoughtless and hurtful words and actions.** (Pause) **"And lead us not into temptation, but deliver us from evil." As we follow you, O God, may we not be tempted to think that we are somehow better than others. Temptation will come, but we ask you to stand with us and give us strength to turn from it and to be delivered from its power.** (Pause) **"For thine is the kingdom, and the power, and the glory, forever." For us to live in your kingdom, in your realm, is to live in your power, and to live in your glorious presence. That life has already begun, and will continue for all time, and beyond all time. Amen. So be it. Amen.** (Pause)

Conclude, **Saying: Be aware of your special place and of Jesus' presence with you. Take a deep breath, and when you are ready, open your eyes.**

78

The Lord's Prayer in Motion

Our Father, who art in heaven,

hallowed be thy name.

Thy kingdom come,
thy will be done

on earth as it is in heaven.

Give us this day our
daily bread.

And forgive us our trespasses,

as we forgive those who
trespass against us.

And lead us not into temptation,

but deliver us from evil

For thine is the kingdom, and the
power, and the glory,

forever.

Amen.

Tithing Event
Stewardship

Stewardship is an integral part of developing a rich spiritual life. Stewardship is about tithing: our money, our time, and our service. During the time of your church's stewardship campaign, host a tithing (stewardship) event for your tweens.

Possible Schedule
1. Opening Activity—A Tithe Is One-Tenth (5 to 10 minutes)
2. Play the Money Game (15 to 20 minutes)
3. Plan Your Church's Budget (25 to 30 minutes)
4. Where Does Your Money Go? (5 to 10 minutes)
   Give a photocopy of the chart on page 85 to each of your tweens and let them work on this exercise individually. Then bring them back together as a group and allow those who wish to do so share information about the difficult decisions they had to make.
5. An Offering for Jerusalem (5 to 10 minutes)
6. Tithe of Your Time (5 minutes)
7. Worship (5 minutes)

A Tithe Is One-Tenth

You will need: pens or pencils, paper.

Talk to your tweens about the concept of tithing.

Say: Since the very beginning, God's people have been expected to return to God a portion of what they gather. Whether it is grain, livestock, or money, God's people are asked to show their appreciation by giving part of it back to its ultimate source, God. A tithe represents the BEST one-tenth of what we have been given. Let's look at how much one-tenth is.

Divide your tweens into groups and let them race to see who gets the answers the quickest.
1. How many feet are in 1/10 of a mile?
2. How much is 1/10 of $75.00?
3. How many hours are in 1/10 of a week?
4. How many people is 1/10 of the population of the United States?

Note: A mile is 5280 feet, and the current population of the United States is about 275,000,000.

Explain that the original concept of tithing goes beyond money. When we tithe, we are thanking God for our existence and prosperity, for our health and family.

Play the Money Game

You will need: photocopy of the cards on either page 83 or page 84, depending upon your church's size; scissors.

Make a photocopy of the role-play cards and then cut them apart. Tell your tweens that they are part of a meeting to determine the budget for your church next year. Pass out the role-play cards to volunteers. Ask the tweens to participate as if they were in a meeting trying to determine the church's budget. After playing the game, discuss the process.

Ask: What things were more difficult to decide about the budget? What things were easier to decide? How do we go about setting priorities for our church's money?

Plan Your Church's Budget

You will need: photocopies of page 87, photocopy of your church's budget for last year.

As a follow up to the above game, or in place of it, pass out copies of the budget form (page 87) and a copy of your church's own budget for last year. Divide the class into groups and give each group a section of the budget form to work on. They are to come up with actual figures for this year's budget. Give them a slight increase or decrease in the amount you think will be pledged. Bring everyone back together and then use consensus to decide upon final figures. You will probably have to stop them before the process is completed.

An Offering for Jerusalem

Read the story of an offering for Jerusalem, Acts 11:19-30. Have your tweens think individually about the following questions. Do not have them share their answers.

Say: Helping other Christians is part of what we are asked to do. How do I do this? What good will my little bit of money do? Will I tithe? Why or why not?

Church members giving 10% or more of their income to God trust God to help them use all of their money wisely so that they will be able to live on the money that is left. Church members who give 10% or more of their time to serve God trust God to help them manage all of their time wisely.

Ask them to remember that what the Antioch church gave to the Jerusalem church was above and beyond what they would normally have given as a tithe. As Christians, much is expected of us.

Tithing Role-Play Cards—1

CUT ALONG DOTTED LINE

You are chair of Staff Parish. One of the young parents in your church has offered to do youth and children's ministries for $10,000 a year. Your church has a few children and even fewer youth, but there are many more in the town that might benefit from this ministry.

You are chair of Trustees. The women's group in your church wants to put a dishwasher in the kitchen for the church suppers that you have once a month. A dishwasher would cost about $500, but it would save more than $500 in paper plates and cups over the course of a year.

You are the parent of two kids, one in seventh grade and one in tenth grade. You like the closeness of being in a small church, but your kids want to go to the church in the next town that has an active youth group.

You are a new member of the church. You joined the church because you liked the way the pastor preached. You would like to get to know some of the other members of the church, but you don't know how.

You are chair of Missions. A group has approached you wanting money for scholarships at the local daycare center. Survivors of a major flood in a neighboring state have asked for money for disaster relief.

You are chair of Finance. The church has had a good year. It looks like next year you will be able to increase your budget by $10,000. You know that some members of the church could give more if they wanted to, but so far you have been unsuccessful in encouraging them to do so.

You are a long-time member of the church. You have been worried that the church was going to die away; but since the new factory came to town, there have been more young families visiting.

You are the parent of a two-year-old and a four-year-old. So far it has not been a problem that there is no Sunday school for your children at your church. However, since the older one is starting to ask questions, you would really like some help in teaching your children about faith. You are not sure that you need to pay anyone, though. Perhaps volunteers could run a program.

Tithing Role-Play Cards—2

You are chair of Staff Parish. Some members of your church would like to have a full-time youth director. Others think you should hire a children's minister. The choir director has requested a part-time organist. Both secretaries want a significant raise, since other church secretaries in the neighborhood receive much more money. What are you going to do?

You are chair of Trustees. The Sunday school committee would like some new tables and chairs for the classrooms. These cost $1,000. The roof over a storage area out back has begun to leak, and it will cost $5,000 to fix it. If you could get volunteers to fix the roof, the materials would cost only $1,000. However, the last time you asked for volunteers, no one showed up.

You are the parent of a two kids, one in seventh grade and one in tenth grade. You don't think the part-time youth director has enough time to do the job. You would like to see the position changed to full-time.

You are a new member of the church. You joined the church because you liked the way the music sounded. You wish the choir director had some help so that the church could have a children's choir and a hand bell choir like your last church did.

You are chair of Missions. A group has approached you wanting $4,000 to help people in the Middle East recover from war. Survivors of a major flood in a neighboring state have asked for $4,000 for disaster relief.

You are chair of Finance. The church has had a good year. It looks like next year you will be able to increase your budget by $50,000. You know that some members of the church could give more if they wanted to, but so far you have been unsuccessful in encouraging them to do so.

You are a long-time member of the church. You have always been excited about the work your church does in local missions—running a food pantry, providing volunteers for the homeless shelter, and providing school supplies for the neighborhood schools.

You are the parent of a two-year-old and a four-year-old. You wish the church had more programming for young children. Right now all you have is Sunday school and vacation Bible school. You would like to see a play group for preschoolers and perhaps after-school care for the neighborhood school.

Where Does Your Money Go?

FILL IN THE TWO PIE CHARTS BELOW.

FIRST, where do you get your money?

WRITE down every place from which you receive money in a month (allowance, money earned from baby-sitting or yard work).

ADD the amounts, then figure out what percentage of your total amount comes from what source.

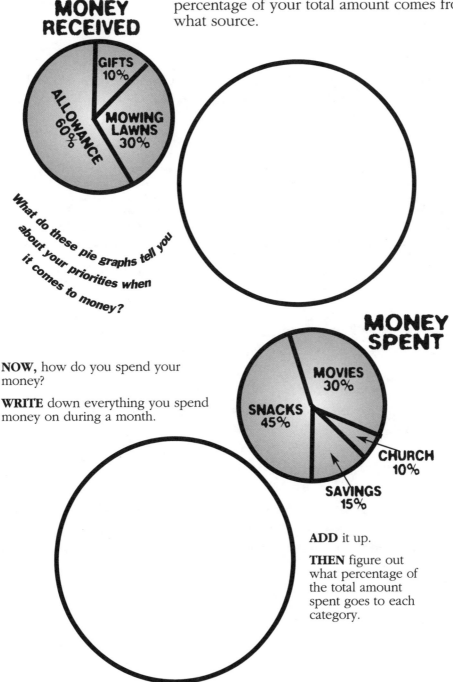

MONEY RECEIVED

- GIFTS 10%
- MOWING LAWNS 30%
- ALLOWANCE 60%

What do these pie graphs tell you about your priorities when it comes to money?

NOW, how do you spend your money?

WRITE down everything you spend money on during a month.

MONEY SPENT

- MOVIES 30%
- SNACKS 45%
- CHURCH 10%
- SAVINGS 15%

ADD it up.

THEN figure out what percentage of the total amount spent goes to each category.

Tithe of Your Time

You will need: two index cards per tween, pens or pencils.

Tithing is not just about money; it is also about time and talent. When we join a church we are asked to commit our presence and our time as well as our tithe.

Have your tweens brainstorm ways they can use their time to be helpful to the church. (Encourage them to think about their talents.)

Give each tween two index cards. Have them choose one of their talents that they will use and a way they personally can use their time for the good of God's kingdom. Have them write these on both cards. Have them then sign one of the cards and bring both cards to worship with them.

Worship

You will need: cards completed in "Tithe of Your Time" activity, cassette/CD of song for closing, cassette/CD player. Optional: offering plate.

Today you are being asked to give a part of yourself to God. This week try as hard as you can to do whatever you wrote on your card.

Ask each tween to come forward during the playing of a closing song and place their signed card face down on the table (or in an offering plate).

Ask the tweens to take their other card home with them and post it in their room as a reminder. Tell them that you will check back next week to see how easy or difficult it was to give the time you tithed.

Close with a prayer of your own, or use this prayer:

Pray: Lord God, we come to you with humble hearts, knowing that all we have belongs to you. Please accept the portion of ourselves that we pledge to return to you. Bless us that we may more fully serve you, now and always. Amen.

Church Budget

Anticipated Income

Expenses

Denominational Required Donations

Staff Salaries
- Pastor
- Administrative Assistant
- Music Director
- Accompanist
- Nursery Worker
- Custodian

Utilities

Insurance

Trustees
- Church Maintenance
- Cleaning Supplies

Office Ministry
- Office Supplies/Paper
- Postage
- Copier
- Telephone
- Computer Expenses

Programs
- Curriculum
- VBS
- Teacher Appreciation
- Youth
- Visitor Follow-up
- Prayer Chain
- Devotionals
- Graduate Gifts
- Bibles for Third Graders
- Missionary Support
- Special Projects
- Communion Supplies
- Bulletins
- Flowers
- Organ Maintenance/Piano Tuning
- Copyright Licensing

Total Budget

Healing Event

Tweens, like adults, have to deal with sickness and death. Those who have been coming to church and Sunday school for a long time have heard more than once the healing stories of Jesus. Talk about different kinds of healing with your tweens—the healing of body, of mind, and of spirit. Use all or some of the following activities to create a healing event for your tweens.

Stories of Healing

You will need: Bibles, paper, pens or pencils.

Divide your class into groups and and assign each group one of the following passages: Matthew 9:27-31; Mark 5:25-34; Luke 5:12-14; 7:11-16; 17:11-19; 18:35-43. (Use only the number of passages appropriate to the size of your group.)

Ask the groups to read the assigned story and answer three questions.
> 1. Who was asking for help and why?
> 2. How did Jesus respond?
> 3. How did those who were healed respond to Jesus?

Each group should select a reporter to report their findings to the rest of the class.

Invite a Healing Panel

You will need: health care professionals for panel.

Most churches have as members (or know of) doctors, nurses, and other health care professionals of faith. Invite three or four of these people to meet with your tween group to talk about what it feels like to be in the health care profession. Encourage them to talk about the times that they can't heal someone as well as the times that they can. (You might want to invite a hospice worker to be a member of the panel.)

Be sure to include a question and answer time.

You might want to prepare your group ahead of time for the panel. Let them work in groups to come up with questions that they would like to have answered.

Visit the Sick

You will need: information about members of your congregation who might appreciate a visit, signed copy of permission slips for each tween (see page 123), transportation, adult chaperones. Optional: pocket crosses (see page 90).

Before your trip gather information from your pastor about people in the church (or people with whom the church is familiar) who would appreciate a visit. Divide the class into groups of three or four and arrange with parents or other adults to transport and chaperone each group. Then give each group the name and address of one person to visit. Arrange for a time to be back at the church. Encourage them to make pocket crosses (see page 90) to give to the person they visit.

Note: Be sure that every tween gives you a signed permission slip BEFORE you take them anywhere.

When each group has returned, together discuss their experience.

Ask: How did you feel before the visit? What was the person you visited like? What were their feelings when you left? What were your feelings after the visit?

Be a Healer Yourself

Let tweens know that they can make a difference in how someone feels.

Suggest that if someone in their home is sick, they can do something as small as getting him or her a glass of orange juice or water and asking with a smile, "Is there anything else I can get for you?" It doesn't cure the person, but helps make him or her more comfortable and less lonely.

If someone is hurting because she or he is lonely or because her or his feelings have been hurt, tell the tweens that they can help that person heal by being a friend.

Here are other ways for tweens to be healers. Ask the tweens to do at least two of the following this week:

• Make a get-well card for someone who is sick or who needs cheering up.
• Think about your own life. How do you show compassion?
• Pray for someone in your community who is sick.
• Pray for people who are healers.

Pocket Crosses

You will need (for each cross): one twelve-inch piece of telephone wire, seven pony beads.

Work with the tweens to make pocket crosses, which can be taken to people your class visits as part of the healing event.

1. Have the tweens thread the telephone wire through the first pony bead, then fold the wire in half.
2. Have the tweens string a total of four pony beads onto the wire. Tell them to be sure that both strands of wire go through the pony beads.
3. Tell the tweens to divide the wires by bending one to the right and one to the left.
4. Have them string a pony bead on the wire on the right, and bend the wire down and thread it back through the bead so it comes out the top. Then have them do the same with the wire on the left.
5. Have the tweens adjust the wire so it begins to look like a cross.
6. Tell them to thread both wires through the last pony bead at the top.
7. Have the tweens thread the remaining pony bead on one wire and thread the other wire through the bead from the other side.
8. Tell the tweens to trim wires to one inch and thread the remaining wire back through the center of the cross.

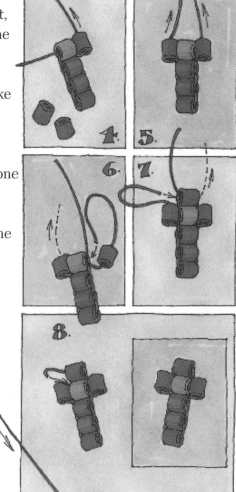

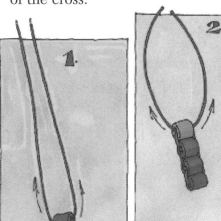

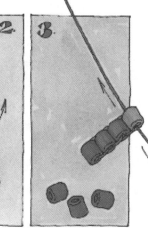

Tween-Led Worship

Post a sign-up sheet for leading worship over the next several weeks. Leave room for three or four tweens to sign up as a team to prepare worship for each session. Make a photocopy of one of the worship suggestions on the following pages (and/or give them a copy also of the sections titled Possible Worship Openings, Song or Hymn Possibilities, and Other possibilities). You might want to come up with your own worship ideas and give them a written copy. They may use these or their own, but you will probably find that most tweens will feel more comfortable using the helps they are given.

CUT ALONG DOTTED LINE

Possible Worship Openings

Use any of the following verses as worship openings: Psalm 118:24, 25, 26, 27, 28, 29; John 4:23-24.

Worship Possibility: Prayer List

Begin a prayer list. Ask if anyone has a concern (that is, a problem or a sickness) about which he or she would like to have everyone pray. List these concerns on a large sheet of paper. Ask if anything very good has happened for which they would like to offer a prayer of thanks. List these people or things on the prayer list.

Pray something like this:

Dear God, Please help those who are sick find strength in your love and care. Be with them now when they need you most. Also, dear God, thank you for all of the wonderful things that happen to us each week. We pray in Jesus' name. Amen.

Worship Possibility: Write and Read a Psalm Litany

Read Psalm 118:25 for the opening.

Write and read a litany. Here is an example of a litany:

Leader: Help us love you more than money.
All: We ask you to be our strength, O Lord!
Leader: Help us love you more than fame.
All: Be our strength, O Lord!
Leader: Help us love you more than winning the ball game.
All: Be our strength, O Lord!
All: Help us look to you for our success. Help us to be happy being your servants. Amen!

CUT ALONG DOTTED LINE

Worship Possibility: Communion Sunday

Pass a loaf of uncut bread around the class. Tell each person to help the person next to him or her by holding the loaf while his or her neighbor tears off a piece to eat; continue this until everyone has torn off a piece. As each person passes the bread, he or she should say, "God loves you."

Note: This is not a true Communion service, but a service of symbolic remembering.

Worship Possibility: Jesus and Prayer

Read one or more of the following Scripture passages about Jesus and prayer while the class bows their heads in silent prayer: Matthew 6:5-6, 7-12; 21:22; Mark 11:25; Luke 3:21-22; 6:12; 9:18a; 22:44-46.

Close with everyone reciting the Lord's Prayer together.

Worship Possibility: Easter

Have an Easter song playing or sing your favorite Easter hymns while you attach real or handmade flowers to an empty cross.

Worship Possibility: Pass the Torch

Before class, make a "torch" (like an Olympic torch). Of course, you will not be able to light it. For the flame, you might want to use newspaper and paint the top yellow, or you might want to use two colors of tissue paper—use your imagination.

Begin your worship by reading 2 Timothy 1:3-5.

Say: We have learned about the love of God and the salvation brought by Jesus through our parents, our teachers, and our older friends. We must keep the flame of faith going. As a symbol of this we will pass the torch around the class.

If you would like to do so, you can sing the song "Pass It On" while the torch is being passed.

Read 2 Timothy 4:7.
Have everyone pray together the Lord's Prayer.

Worship Possibility: Hold a "Speak Boldly" Rally

Read Acts 4:20.

Give everyone a large sheet of paper and a marker. Ask each person to write a cheer on his or her paper. For example:

"You can do it!"

"God loves you!"

"Hooray!"

When everyone has finished, ask each person to take a turn making a bold statement about what wonderful things God has allowed us to see or hear in this world. After each bold statement have everyone cheer by using the words of encouragement from the large sheets of paper. Use streamers and confetti and do a lot of jumping around as you would at a school pep rally.

Worship Possibility: Commit to Pray

Ask your teacher for a Scripture from today's lesson. As part of worship, read the selected Scripture.

Give everyone in your class four slips of paper and a pencil. Have them write a name of a friend on each slip of paper and then fold the slips of paper so no one can see the names they have written.

Say: This week we are going to pray for our friends. Think about the names you wrote on your slips of paper. This week commit to pray for one or more of those friends. Think about the people for whom you will commit to pray. You may pray for one or all four of the friends whose names you wrote, but if you commit to pray for them, you are expected to carry through with your commitment.

Show them where they are to put their slips of paper—for example, in a bowl, in a prayer box, on the prayer post. If you don't have any specific place, just put a plate or basket on the worship table.

Ask your classmates to put the names for which they have committed to pray in the place they have been shown. They may put whatever slips of paper they care to keep in their pocket so that no one knows for how many people they are going to pray.

Pray: God we thank you for our friends. Keep them safe and well. Help make us better friends. Amen.

CUT ALONG DOTTED LINE

Worship Possibility: Write a Song, Prayer, or Litany

Write a song, prayer, or litany and present it to the class, or perform a Bible story as a drama.

Worship Possibility: Apostles' Creed

Ask your teacher for a copy of the Apostles' Creed. (It is in some hymnals.) Copy the creed onto a large sheet of paper or type it out on the computer and print out several copies and hand them out to worshipers.

For worship, lead everyone in the Apostles' Creed. Close with a prayer. You may choose one from a prayer resource that your teacher provides or make up your own prayer.

Worship Possibilities: Advent Wreath and Litanies

Use the worship that comes in your weekly curriculum or an Advent worship booklet to lead the worship for your week in Advent. Light the correct number of candles on the Advent wreath.

Worship Possibility: Light of the World

Decorate the worship table with as many kinds of light as you can: candles, flashlights, lamps. Write a litany about light. (Ask your teacher for a sample of a litany.)

Start worship by reading John 8:12. Lead a song with the word *light* in it, such as "Thy Word" or "This Little Light of Mine." End with a prayer. You may choose one from a prayer resource that your teacher provides, or you may make up your own prayer.

Song or Hymn Possibilities

Use your church's hymnal to find a hymn you like. Ask if you can use a few of the hymnals in your classroom during class. Return them immediately to the sanctuary when class is finished. If you are musical, make up a song. Sing a song for the class, or have everyone sing a song together.

Other Possibilities

Look at your denomination's book of worship or prayer book for more ideas.

Congregational Life

Offering opportunities
for meaningful
participation in
the life of the
congregation is
essential to the spiritual
growth of tweens.

Congregational Life

Christian spirituality is most often corporate. There are times we must withdraw, as Jesus did, to pray and listen for the Word of God; but, as with Jesus, most spiritual disciplines take place within the community of faith.

• Parents, Christian educators, Sunday school teachers, significant mentors—all of these people must be **seen** worshiping together. Tweens learn best by observing behavior. A tween's radar is very good—they can spot the difference between "talkin' the talk" and "walkin' the walk" very quickly.

• Tweens **must** be given significant ways to participate in the life of the congregation and in corporate worship.

• Different church environments and church sizes may call for different approaches.

• Tweens need to be known by and greeted by name. Younger children get lots of attention because they are cute. By the time children become tweens they have become "invisible" to the congregation unless they have done something that gets them into trouble. Encourage intentional personal relationships with adult members of the congregation.

Activities

Signs of Prayer

Have your tweens read this litany in words and in American Sign Language for congregational worship.

CUT ALONG DOTTED LINE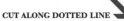

My Prayer, Our Prayer

Reader 1: God, you are kind and loving. You are always with us.

All: Hear our prayer, O Lord. (signing)

Reader 2: God, we often fail you by cheating, lying, or hurting other people. We are sorry. Please forgive our sins.

All: Hear our prayer, O Lord. (signing)

Reader 3: God, our world cannot survive without our help. We need food, clothing, and shelter. We need people who care about us.

All: Hear our prayer, O Lord. (signing)

Reader 4: God, all around the world there are people who are hurting. Some are sick. Others are hungry. Some have no place to call home.

All: Hear our prayer, O Lord. (signing)

Reader 5: God, thank you for giving us this day. Thank you for this church and the people in our class.

All: Hear our prayer, O Lord. (signing)

Reader 6: God, we pray these prayers asking that your will be done. Amen.

HEAR
Form the letter "C" with your right hand and cup it against your ear.

OUR
Slightly cup your right hand and place the thumb against your right shoulder. Circle your hand around until your little finger touches your left shoulder.

PRAYER
Place your hands together as shown. Then pull your hands toward your body, slightly bowing your head at the same time.

O
Hold the right hand in the shape of an "O" as shown.

LORD
With your right hand at your left shoulder, form the letter "L." Now, move your hand across the chest to your waist.

Stage a Magnificent March

You will need: Bibles, posterboard, markers, construction paper, permission from pastor.

During Advent, have the tweens design and create signs that express the magnificent things that God has done and is doing in their lives and in the life of the church. Use half-sheets of posterboard for each sign. Encourage them to use lots of color—either with colored markers or with shapes cut from colored construction paper.

Have them prepare a chant based on one or more verses from Luke 1:46-55. For example, "A song of praise my spirit sings—the Mighty One has done great things!" or "Holy is the Mighty One, cared enough to send a Son!"

Carrying their signs and doing their chant, have the tweens march throughout the church building to magnify God before the congregation. Or, they may want to sing Christmas carols as they march.

Note: A march could also be done as a celebration at other times during the year.

Sharing Our Story Exhibition

You will need: art supplies, Bibles.

There are so many different ways to share messages in today's world that everyone should be able to find a way to share God's Word. Have your tweens think about the message they want to share. Let them create a class art exhibit to share the message.

Have each tween choose an art form in which to present his or her message—sculpture, paint, line drawing, woodwork, computer-generated art, and so forth. The class can choose to all highlight the same Bible verse or theme, or they might individually choose a Bible verse or theme that their art will illustrate. Have them work on that project.

You will want to give the tweens at least three to four weeks for this project. If your church does not have art supplies on hand, they will need to be gathered; or the tweens may choose to do their artwork at home using their own supplies.

Check with your pastor to locate a place where you can have your "exhibit hall." Invite everyone in the church to come see the exhibits the tweens have developed. Publicize the event by having the tweens write an article for the newsletter, post an add on the church web page, and put up posters around the church. You might even want to sponsor a "Tea and Exhibition" at a time other than Sunday morning when your tweens can be present with their exhibits and people can come to see them.

Buddy Class Projects

Become a Buddy Class or Group

You will need: list of adult classes and groups in your church, large piece of posterboard, markers.

Talk with your tweens about one way that they can make the world a better place: in their personal relationships. Explain how they might have to be the ones to take the first steps to reach out and learn more about other people and show them God's love.

Ask them to work together to choose one adult class or group in the church to reach out to and with which to become "buddies." For the rest of the quarter or year, work on doing things for and with a Buddy Class or Buddy Group. (For the purpose of simplicity, the Buddy Class or Group from this point on will be referred to as the "Buddy Class.")

Let the tweens offer suggestions as to which adult class they want to be their Buddy Class. Encourage them to choose a class with people they don't know well or people who might need a "buddy," such as a young adult class (who may not have children yet), an older adult class, or a special needs class. Be sure that you get a list of the names of the members of your Buddy Class.

Have the class work together on an oversized note for their Buddy Class that announces your class' intention of adopting their class. This oversized card can be made by using a large sheet of posterboard, either flat or folded. Let the class design the card and write the message, and make sure that everyone signs the card.

Use the projects on pages 100-102 or invent your own to enjoy a year with a Buddy Class.

Make a Buddy Class Collage

You will need: craft supplies and/or camera and film.

You can make a collage for your Buddy Class in one of several ways:

• Have the tweens draw "self-portraits," label each portrait with his or her name, and paste the self-portraits of the entire class on a large sheet of posterboard.

• Take a photo of each tween and tape the photos on a piece of posterboard. Label the photos.

• Take a photo of the tweens and have them make frames for their photos. Have them measure their photos and cut construction paper to extend about an inch past the photo on all sides, cutting a photo-sized opening in the center of the frame. Decorate the frame. Place each photo on a piece of posterboard and glue it into place, then place the frame around the picture and glue it down. When dry, trim the posterboard to the size of the frame, and attach all the framed photos to a large sheet of posterboard.

When your collage is finished (this may take more than one class session), go as a class to present it to your Buddy Class.

Hold a Party for Your Buddy Class

You will need: posterboard and marker for brainstorming, party supplies and food for party.

Plan a party for your Buddy Class. Have a brainstorming session to decide what you will do at the party and make assignments to complete all the necessary preparations. Record the ideas and assignments on a posterboard.

Possible assignments:
> • check suggested dates for the party with Buddy Class and report back
> • make table decorations and/or party favors
> • food
> • music
> • intergenerational games (get acquainted games might be a good idea)

Interview Buddy Class

Pair up one or more tweens with one or more members of the Buddy Class. It's nice if the tweens can choose, but you might have to give them a second or third choice if too many want to pair up with the same buddy.

Arrange a convenient time with your Buddy Class to sit down together and let the tweens interview their buddies about their faith experiences.

You might need to provide your tweens with some questions to ask.

Attend Worship with Buddy Class

Make arrangements for your Buddy Class to sit with the tweens during worship. The two groups should mingle, with tweens and adults sitting mixed together instead of all of the tweens in one row and all of the adults in another.

Go On a Buddy Class Picnic

You will need: sign up sheet, signed copy of permission slip for each tween (see page 123), food.

Agree on a date with your Buddy Class to go on a joint picnic (in nice weather, of course). Depending upon the Buddy Class, you may or may not have to make arrangements for transportation. (Many older adults or special needs adults may not be able to drive.) In any case, you will need permission slips for transporting tweens.

Have a sign up sheet for food with every tween and every adult providing something for the picnic.

Serve Together

You will need: large sheet of paper or dry erase board and markers for brainstorming, other items depending upon the service project selected.

Bring the tweens and the Buddy Class together for a meeting. Let them brainstorm possible service projects in which both groups could participate.

Let the entire group then vote on which service project they wish to complete. Follow through with the project, making sure that every tween and adult has a way to participate in the service project.

Prepare Worship for Buddy Class

You will need: tween-led worship helps (see pages 91-94), Bibles.
Optional: cassette/CD player, musical instruments.

Using the tween-led worship helps on pages 91-94, let your tweens prepare a short worship experience for your Buddy Class. Check with the class or group as to which Sunday morning (or meeting time—perhaps you're doing this on Wednesday or Sunday nights) would be best for the presentation of this tween-led worship experience.

Best Friends Chat

During class time or over lunch pair up (or put in small groups) tweens and members of the Buddy Class. Start by letting a Buddy Class member in each group talk for a few minutes about his or her best friend and what it is like to have a best friend. Encourage each tween to share with his or her buddy about his or her own best friend.

Co-Sponsor a Christmas Project

You will need: list of possible projects, wrapping paper, scissors, tape, Christmas tags, items to be brought in and/or purchased by participants.

There are opportunities everywhere in the country to make or buy Christmas presents for disadvantaged persons—either children or adults. Get your tweens and Buddy Class together to choose someone to sponsor. You might have to do some research ahead of time. It is possible that your Buddy Class will know of needs, or perhaps your church is involved already in projects within which your groups could work.

Just how many people or what kinds of project your group selects will depend largely on the size and financial capabilities of your group. One idea is to go Christmas shopping together and/or all work together to wrap the presents gathered.

Feed Your Buddy Class

You will need: food (depending upon what you decide to serve), plates, napkins, cups, eating utensils, location for meal.

Set a date for after (or before) a regular meeting time and have your tweens serve lunch (or dinner) to your Buddy Class. Make it something simple that tweens can do without chopping off fingers or burning down the building.

Sample menu: sandwiches, chips, a raw vegetable tray (many vegetables come precut), and cookies or brownies (most tweens can make cookies or brownies, but don't leave the oven unsupervised). Let the tweens set the table, serve the meal, and clean up.

Take a "Tacky Light" Tour

You will need: transportation, signed copy of permission slip for each tween (see page 123).

Gather together some cars and vans from the church and take your tweens and Buddy Class on a "Tacky Light" tour at Christmas.

Note: Encourage your Buddy Class to suggest some times to spend together. Most classes will not need any encouragement, but others may. Don't let this be a time where the tweens do all the serving. Let this project encourage mutual respect and participation.

More Congregational Life Activities

Worship Bulletin

Examine a Worship Bulletin

You will need: worship bulletins.

Give each tween a copy of this week's worship bulletin. Have the tweens identify places where worship appears to be done by only one person or by a small group. Help the tweens realize that at such times, everyone in the service is invited to be involved. For instance, when only one person is praying aloud, all are invited to pray silently; when the choir is singing, all are invited to think about the words and music.

Help the tweens identify the number of times the Bible is used in the service. Look for obvious uses such as reading from the Scripture. If your congregation uses readings each week from both the Old Testament and the New Testament, emphasize that to your tweens.

Look for less obvious uses of the Bible. Help the tweens realize that responsive readings are often from the Bible, that the Lord's Prayer is recorded in the Bible, that many hymns are based on Scripture, and that sermons are based on Scripture.

Encourage the tweens to take their personal Bibles into the worship service. Suggest that they silently read Psalm 122:1 from their Bibles at the beginning of the worship service.

Create Worship Bulletin Covers

You will need: Bible, permission for the project, list of Scripture references, paper, markers and/or paints.

Get permission from your pastor and worship committee for the tweens of the church to create worship bulletin covers. Good times of the year to do this project may be during the Lenten, Advent, Christmas, and Epiphany seasons. These times lend themselves to more covers being used; therefore, more tweens could participate.

Get a list of the Scriptures for the specified weeks from your pastor. Have the tweens discuss and think about the Scriptures. Let them choose which one they wish to illustrate; or encourage them to do illustrations of more than one, and then let the group decide which ones will be submitted for use on the cover of the worship bulletins. If your church has a color copier, have them do their work in color. If not, have them do their work in black marker. (They may work in pencil and then go over it with a black marker. Pencil alone will not copy well.)

Church Newsletter

Compose Letters of Encouragement

You will need: paper, pens or pencils.

Remind your tweens that Paul wrote letters of advice to several churches. The letters were written to encourage the churches.

Suggest that your tweens write words of encouragement to your congregation. Plan to photocopy the letters and let the tweens distribute the letters of encouragement to members of your congregation next Sunday. You could put these letters in the church newsletter over a period of weeks or months, you could distribute them when the Scripture is read during the worship service, or you could include them as an insert in next Sunday's worship bulletin. Be sure to get approval for your plan from your pastor.

Drum Up Support for Missions

You will need: paper, pens or pencils.

If your tweens are doing a missions project, have them advertise it in the church newsletter. If they have completed a service project, encourage them to work together to write an article for the church newsletter about what they did and what they experienced.

Submit Prayers

You will need: permission from editor of church newsletter, paper, pens or pencils.

Check with whoever is in charge of newsletter content for permission to print prayers written by your tweens.

Have a session on prayer with your tweens and give them time to write prayers (or let them bring a prayer at a later time). Encourage the newsletter to either devote a page to the prayers or to print some of the prayers in each of the next few newsletters, whichever is most appropriate to the space and type of newsletter your church produces.

If your church has a web-based newsletter, it should be easy to add a space for prayers written by tweens.

World Communion Sunday Event

Bring tweens and adults together for an intergenerational event that will make this day special for all of them. Choose some or all of the following activities to make World Communion Sunday more meaningful.

Read the Bible Together

You will need: Bibles.

At the beginning of your time together read one of the stories of the institution of the Lord's Supper to the group as the opening worship: Matthew 26:26-30; Mark 14:22-25; Luke 22:14-23; 1 Corinthians 11:23-26.

Remember Members Who Live Far Away

Need: paper, pens or pencils, envelopes, stamps, felt-tip markers, U.S. or world map.

Ask your church office for the names and addresses of church members who do not live near your church. Choose several from around the country and around the world. Invite the participants to write letters of greeting to these church members.

Post a U.S. or world map on the wall. Have participants write on the map with a felt-tip marker the names of church members to whom you are writing greetings.

Bake and Present Communion Bread

You will need: ingredients (see list below), mixing bowls and utensils, baking sheet.

Make arrangements with your pastor or worship committee for the participants to make Communion bread and to bring the bread forward for presentation at the church's Communion service. (You can freeze this bread until the next Communion service.) You may want to use the following recipe to make your Communion bread.

Ingredients: ¾ cup butter, ¾ cup sugar, ¼ teaspoon salt, 1 cup sour milk or add 1 tablespoon vinegar to 1 cup milk, ¼ teaspoon baking soda, 1 teaspoon baking powder, 4 cups all-purpose flour, flour for kneading.

Preheat the oven to 350 degrees. Stir butter and sugar together until consistency is creamy. Add the remaining ingredients in the order listed. Mix well. Give each participant a golf-ball-sized piece of dough. Shape the dough into flat loaves on a floured surface. Place each loaf on a baking sheet. Bake at 350 degrees for ten to fifteen minutes. Let cool before eating. Makes 24 to 28 small loaves.

Communion Service Project

You will need: pastor or other church representative, items to serve Communion.

Ask your pastor to plan a time when your class can join the pastor (or other representative from your church) in serving Communion to a person who is homebound. Set up a time to have the server talk about the importance of serving Communion to someone who is homebound. Encourage the participants to talk with the recipient about what being able to take Communion means to him or her.

After the trip give time for the participants to "debrief" with the Communion server. Let them ask any questions that they may have about serving Communion to other people who can't come to church—those who work, those who may be sick, and so forth.

Create a Liturgical Dance

You will need: copy of your church's Communion liturgy.

Tell the participants that you will be reading the words that are sometimes used when the bread is broken at Communion. As they hear these words, they are to create movements that they personally think would go with the words. For example:

> The pastor breaks the bread.
> The people receive the bread.
> The pastor lifts the cup.
> The people receive the wine.
> The congregation sings hymns while the bread and cup are given.
> When all have received, the Lord's Table is put in order.

Look up your church's Communion liturgy in your hymnal or worship bulletin and read it to the tweens. Let them use the motions inspired by these words to create a liturgical dance.

Service Around the World

You will need: list with addresses of Christian organizations that need help; world map; dry erase board and erasable marker, chalkboard and chalk, or large sheet of paper and marker.

Note: Before this event ask the pastor and/or the person in charge of world missions in your church to help you find a list (with addresses) of Christian organizations around the world that need help. Make copies of this information.

If you do not have a world map posted where everyone can see it, do so for this activity.

Divide the participants into groups of four or five. Give each group a copy of the information you have gathered on Christian organizations around the world. Give each group fifteen minutes to choose three projects they think are worthy of helping. They are come to this decision by consensus. Let each group choose one of the tweens to report back.

Caution: If there are too many adults in a group, the tweens will not talk freely. Put either an equal number of tweens and adults or more tweens than adults in a group.

After fifteen minutes bring the groups back together. Have each group mark on the world map where the projects on their list are located. This gives everyone a visual image of where the projects are located.

Then on a dry erase board, chalkboard, or large sheet of paper, record the projects that each group has chosen as they are reported. Together look over the lists and see if there are any that are the same. Put a star or checkmark beside any duplicates. These will automatically appear on your list as you narrow it down.

Allow all of the participants to discuss the projects and narrow them down to five (three if you have only two groups). As you discuss the projects, make sure that you consider what your group will do to support the project (for example, fundraising or gathering materials to send to the project will probably be involved). Then go through the list again, discuss the projects, and narrow the list down to two projects. Then vote on the final project.

Together make a list of things that must be done to accomplish what you want to do. Keeping everyone in the original groups, give every group an assignment (volunteering is much more energizing than just appointing someone).

Put someone in charge of making sure that the project actually happens. In the coming days or weeks, carry out the project.

Worship

You will need: hymnals, Bibles.

Close the World Communion Sunday event with worship. Chose a favorite Communion hymn. Read again the story of the institution of Communion from the Bible, and close with a prayer.

Churchwide Reconciliation Day

You will need: permission from pastor. Optional: supplies to make badges (computer, printer, badge-maker), information booth and fliers.

Ask the pastor if tweens can sponsor a Churchwide Reconciliation Day. Be sure to get permission before starting this activity.

Use Matthew 7:12 (the Golden Rule) as the theme for the day. One possible activity is to make badges for the congregation to wear. Use a computer to print the words and graphics, have the tweens cut out the paper for the badges, and use a badge-maker to make them into wearable badges.

Sponsor an information booth in honor of the day; at the booth provide informational fliers on Christian conflict resolution for the congregation.

Have the tweens prepare and give a children's sermon. Give each child who comes a badge with the Golden Rule printed on it.

Prepare Blessing of the Animals Service

You will need: copy of Blessing of the Animals Service, permission from pastor.

Speak with your pastor and worship committee before meeting with the tweens to get approval for this activity.

Walk the tweens through the "Blessing of the Animals" service. Many churches have this service in their books of worship or other worship materials. If the tweens will be helping in the service, help them plan their part of the service and help them assign parts. Practice the service.

Have them write an announcement for the church newsletter and a special letter to be mailed to the congregation that announces the special service and asks people to bring their pets.

Giving Back

Take your tweens on an exploration of your own church building to look for ways people have helped to build your church. Tell them to look for things that are available because people have given their talents.

Tour the church (inside and outside, if possible). Encourage the tweens to point out the things they see that indicate people have given of their talents. Some are things people use their talents to build or give; others are things that people use their talents during the week and donate the money to give. You might point out such things as musical instruments, equipment in the kitchen, tables and chairs in Sunday school areas, altar cloths, hymnals, carpet, sidewalks, parking lots, playground equipment, and plants.

As you tour, encourage the tweens to think about ways they can help provide things the church needs. Things that tweens can do include sharpening pencils for the sanctuary, picking up litter, washing nursery toys, dusting pews, helping prepare bread and juice for Communion, serving as an acolyte, ushering, singing in the children's choir, pledging a part of their allowance, praying, inviting someone to church, and participating in churchwide service projects.

Make Blessing Cards

You will need: construction paper and markers or computer, printer, and printer paper; envelopes; stamps.

Identify persons in your congregation who have been involved in outreach ministries and make cards to give or send to these persons, affirming what they have done or are doing. You can make these cards from construction paper or use the computer to make the cards.

The outside of the card might say, "You that are blessed, you that are a blessing," and the inside contain the following:

"Inherit the kingdom prepared for you from the foundation of the world; for I was hungry and you gave me food, I was thirsty and you gave me something to drink, I was a stranger and you welcomed me, I was naked and you gave me clothing, I was sick and you took care of me, I was in prison and you visited me" (Matthew 25:34-36). Thank you for all you do.

Make a Stole for the Pastor

You will need: cloth, scissors, thread, needles or sewing machine, adult with sewing experience and patience. Optional: felt, fabric paints.

A great way for tweens to give back to the church in a meaningful way is to make a stole for the pastor. You will want to include someone with a sewing machine and some talent sewing to help with this project.

Let your tweens help with as many steps as you think they can handle (depending upon their ability and the patience of the person handling the sewing instructions and machine).

1. Cut four pieces of cloth, each 45-inches long by 6-inches wide.

2. Put two of the pieces together with the right sides together. Sew across one end to form a strip that is 6-inches wide and about 90-inches long when opened. Repeat with the other two strips to form a second 90-inch strip.

3. Press the seams open.

4. Place the two 90-inch strips together with right sides together. Match the seams. Sew around the long edges and one end of the fabric. Leave one end open.

5. Turn the stole right-side-out through the open end. Press the stole.

6. Turn about ½-inch of the raw edges of the open end to the inside and press. Hand stitch the open end closed.

Let your tweens decorate the stole using fabric paints and symbol shapes cut from felt. As a group present the stole to the pastor on her or his birthday; or, if there is a staff appreciation day at your church, make arrangements for your group to present the stole at that time.

Family

Tweens are struggling with questioning their faith and making their faith their own. This is a time when tweens are pulling away. As parents, allow your tweens some breathing room to discover their own faith.

At the same time, remember tweens are not adults or even older youth! Tweens need adult direction! Now is not the appropriate time to give tweens a choice about church. It is crucial at this juncture to worship together as a family.

Parents

- **Model, Model, Model!**—Tweens must see their parents practice spiritual disciplines, if they are to develop spiritual lives of their own. (Tweens still learn more from modeling and practicing than from any other method.)

- **Attend Sunday School and Church Regularly as a Family!**
    - When parents drop a tween off at church and then go to breakfast, this teaches the tween that spiritual matters are insignificant for adults.
    - Giving a tween a choice between spirituality and sleeping or going to the ball game teaches the tween that a relationship with God and other Christians is an option and of secondary importance.

- **Read**—If your tween's curriculum has a parent newsletter or parent page, read it. If you have not been receiving one, ask your tween's Sunday school teacher if one exists. It will help you parent your tween spiritually.

- **Continue Special Worship Events From Early Childhood**
    - Say grace before mealtimes. (Actually eat some meals together each week. Studies show it's important to family relationships and to the learning of values.)
    - If you read the Christmas story as a family or go to Christmas Eve services together, continue to do so.
    - If you have a special devotional time as a family, let your tween take charge of the devotional time, at least sometimes.

- **. It Is Not Too Late to Start Special Home Devotional Times!**
    - Light Advent candles.
    - Read the Bible as a family.
    - Say grace at meals.
    - Set aside a special corner for devotions and prayer.

- **Answer Spiritual Questions Honestly**
    - Talk about Sunday school over Sunday lunch or in the car on the way to Sunday lunch.
    - If you need help, ask for it—from your pastor, Christian educator, or other respected Christian. (It is okay to allow your tweens to know you don't know the answer to everything.)
    - Never pretend to understand something you don't. You will lose credibility with your tween.

- **Pray for Your Tween Daily**

Nurturing Your Family's Spiritual Life

We tend to think we need a lot of solitude and space to grow spiritually. Not so. There are many creative ways family members can grow spiritually. Consider these ideas:

• *Expand your prayer times*—When do you pray as a family? At mealtimes? bedtimes? Create other times to pray, such as on Sunday evenings to ask God to guide each family member as tweens start the school week and adults start the work week. After you watch the news, pray about what you saw. Place names of friends and relatives in a jar; pull a name out each week and pray for that person.

• *Talk, talk, talk*—Tell stories about how your ancestors and other family members stuck with their faith when life was easy—and hard. Talk about your faith journey, your doubts, your meaningful Christian experiences. Ask questions about the faith journey of each family member. Answer questions (and go searching for answers when you don't know them). Make faith an everyday part of conversation.

• *Create religious rituals*—On Pentecost Sunday have everyone in your family wear something red to church. On warm days take a family hike; look for God's creation and the ways people both enhance and destroy that creation. Light candles after you say a mealtime prayer and invite God's presence to surround your family.

• *Attend worship together*—Tweens learn that worshiping God is important when families make it a point to attend worship services on a regular basis. Going to church together also emphasizes how essential it is to be part of a community of faith.

• *Become bigger givers*—Make a giving box or jar into which each family member can place coins. If you're not already in the habit, encourage every member of your family to give a separate contribution to your church.

• *Have quiet times*—Have family members take a quiet time with God. They can pray, read the Bible, be still and listen, or read a Christian book. Set aside some quiet time for God—even if it's just for fifteen minutes a day.

• *Make spirituality fun*—As you eat dinner, see how many women in the Bible your family members can name collectively (without peeking). Invite over a family from church (or a friend from your tween's Sunday school class). Choose a different spot to sit in each week when you go to worship so that your tween can see what it's like to worship from the balcony, the front row, the last row, and the middle of the church. Make your family's spirituality truly an adventure and something everyone is curious to explore.

Written by Jolene L. Roehlkepartain

Family Worship

The start of a new year or the start of a new school year are great times to think about ways that God can be present in our family and our home each day. When we start each day off with God, our days mean more. Family spirituality is important to the life of a Christian. When we sit down and consider our faith journey, most of us find that our family has played a large role in this journey. God called us to be Christians in community. The community includes our family. We need to hear each other pray. We need to speak prayers for others. We need to know that God is with us in our family and in our daily walk.

How do we become a more spiritual family? As a family, we should be attending church together, looking around the community for ways we can share God's love together, talking about Bible stories and Christ's life together, and sharing with each other our love of God.

One helpful way to tell the Bible stories and share our love of God with each other is to set up a family worship center. When we set aside a place in our home for God, then we invite God to be a part of our family and our activities. Setting up space for God in our home can be a fun family project. Start by finding a place in your home—perhaps the dining room table or a small table in the family room. This place should be someplace where the entire family feels comfortable. Once you have a space, set up the worship center. As a family, decide what should be in the worship space—maybe a cross, flowers from the garden, leaves from the trees outside, a Bible. All the items in the worship center should have meaning to you as Christians and as a family.

Now that you have a worship center set up, what should you do? You can make the family worship center the center of your family life by establishing a routine of worship. You may want to have family devotionals each evening, or you may want to light a candle in the mornings before breakfast and say, "Thank you, God, for this beautiful day!"

Family worship is important in the lives of Christians. As Christians we learn how to worship by watching others. When we gather as a family to pray, to be quiet, to read the Scriptures, and to be present with God, we teach each other about our faith. Family worship leads to a deeper understanding of God's love in our lives, most especially for children, even tweens.

Written by Leigh Meekins.

Missions That Families Can Do Together

"I like to volunteer because our whole family is spending time together," says 11-year-old Apolinar, Jr. "The thing that I learned the most is that my family is the most important thing in my life," says 13-year-old Teresa. "I know they're great because they're always helping others."

Apolinar, Jr. and Teresa participate in mission and service projects with their parents Apolinar and Christina Yanez and their 6-year-old sister, Marisol. They've helped clean up the Los Angeles River and participated in projects to raise funds for children and adults with disabilities. By working together, the family has talked more about values and beliefs. The children say they want to continue helping others.

Here are a few ideas to help you and your family get started in a mission project:

- *Choose projects that have appeal to all family members.* Mission projects have a greater impact on each family member when every family member feels included. If a parent goes alone to buy raisins for a food bank, other family members miss out. If a parent wants to help build a house for Habitat for Humanity and none of the children in the family are teenagers yet, the children aren't allowed to contribute because they're too young. Find projects where everyone can have a meaningful role, such as a walk-a-thon. Consider, for example, the annual CROP WALK for Church World Service (28606 Phillips St., P.O. Box 968, Elkhart, IN 46515; 800-297-1516; www.churchworldservice.org).

- *Discuss the scriptural emphasis on mission.* The Bible emphasizes generosity, service, compassion, mission, and justice as priorities for people of faith. As a family, study passages such as Deuteronomy 15:7-8; Micah 6:8; Matthew 6:21; 25:34-35, 40; and Luke 21:1-4. Talk about the value of helping others.

- *Find creative activities.* Families can get bored doing mission projects if new ones aren't introduced periodically. Collect pennies to donate to Common Cents® New York (104 West 88th Street, New York, NY 10024; phone: 212-PENNIES; www.commoncents.org). Make holiday gift boxes for children in other countries for Operation Christmas Child (Samaritan's Purse, P.O. Box 3000, Boone, NC 28607; 800-353-5949; www.samaritanspurse.org).

- *Go deeper.* Families can become mission-minded families by collecting items for a worthy cause, by giving money to important efforts, and by doing projects that directly serve recipients. Most families do well in one of these three areas. How can you strengthen and expand your family's acts of service?

- *Talk about your experience.* Whenever you participate in a mission project, debrief everyone about the experience afterward. Don't assume that all family members had a positive experience or that the project didn't raise any questions. By talking together you'll become closer and learn how to make your next mission experience more meaningful.

CAUTION: Never visit a web site unless you know it's a good site. Also, remember that web addresses can often change.

Written by Jolene L. Roehlkepartain.

Thankful Traditions

Most Fall quarter Sunday school material ends with a celebration of thanksgiving. This is appropriate, because it is often the Sunday just before or after the American celebration of Thanksgiving Day. Thanksgiving Day was made a national holiday in 1863 (during the United States Civil War) by President Abraham Lincoln. (You should get a copy of his full Thanksgiving Day proclamation and read it if you never have—it's very enlightening.)

Giving thanks to God in all ways and at all times is always appropriate. It is very difficult to do so in times of crisis (personal or national) or in times of mourning, but that is what we are called upon to do—give thanks for our Creator and for all we have.

How do we make this "thankfulness" so much a part of our tweens' spiritual lives that it becomes natural for them? It can be done through tradition, practice, and example. Thanksgiving Day dinner with family and attending Thanksgiving church services are a part of building a tradition. But there are other ways to add to this tradition of thankfulness.

One sixth-grader told me that his family has steak for Thanksgiving dinner. I asked why, and he explained that his immediate family always makes Thanksgiving Day dinner for people who are homeless and sits down to eat with them. He said his parents know that steak was something people who are homeless don't often get to eat, so they always fix steak for Thanksgiving dinner! To this sixth grader, eating a steak dinner with people who are homeless is as natural as traveling a hundred miles to sit down to a turkey dinner with family. This is truly a thankful tradition.

Remember that giving thanks to God should not be a tradition limited to one day a year, nor should it center exclusively on thankfulness for food. To produce a thankful tween, you must first be truly thankful for your own relationship with God all year, through good times and bad.

Here are some ways to foster thankfulness in your tween:

- Say a prayer of thanks over every meal.

- As a family, give your time and service to others in thankfulness for your relationship with God.

- Talk about happy things when doing things with your tween—as you travel, as you work together, even as you do the dishes!

- Do not complain continually about what is "wrong with the world" or about what you don't have. Continual complaining is often done not because something is wrong, but because it's a habit. If you try it, speaking thankfully can become a habit.

Keep in mind that children model the behavior of their parents. Model being thankful by being truly thankful yourself.

Written by Marcia Stoner.

Family Activities
Table Grace Card

You will need: 3- by 5-inch unlined index cards, markers, scissors.

Blessing: a gift from God.
Grace: a short prayer of thanksgiving, said before or after a meal.

When people love and serve God, they remember to give thanks for God's blessings. Use these ideas to work together with your tween to make a table grace card for your family to use as a beginning to mealtime prayers. Have everyone in your family make a card. Rotate using the cards.

Cut a 2- by 4-inch rectangle in the middle of a 3- by 5-inch unlined index card. You now have a frame. Use felt-tip markers to draw fruits, vegetables, grains, or flowers on the frame.

On a separate index card, print a favorite Bible verse. Make sure you keep your writing in the center of the card so that the frame will not cover it up. You might choose from one of the following:

The earth has yielded its increase; God, our God, has blessed us. (Psalm 67:6)

O LORD my God, I will give thanks to you forever. (Psalm 30:12b)

Then we your people, the flock of your pasture, will give thanks to you forever. (Psalm 79:13a)

Rejoice in the LORD, O you righteous, and give thanks to his holy name! (Psalm 97:12)

Tape one edge of the frame to the Bible verse card. Stand the table grace card in the center of your dining table at home.

Napkin Rings

You will need: construction paper, scissors, clear adhesive paper, stapler, markers.

Together cut strips for napkin rings from construction paper (the easiest and cheapest way to do this) and have your tween write a Bible verse on each one. Then decorate each napkin ring, cover it with clear adhesive paper, and staple the two ends together. Make several (more than there are family members). Then each time the family shares an evening or Sunday noon meal have someone read the Bible verse on his or her napkin ring. Include the thoughts from that verse in the blessing for the day. When the napkin rings wear out, make more with new verses.

Our Daily Bread

Throughout the Bible bread is used as a symbol of the very central need of life. This is true literally in the need for sustaining the physical body, but it is also true for spiritual sustainment. In Communion, bread is used to represent the physical body ("This is my body" Mark 14:22), and Jesus calls himself "the bread of life" (John 6:35). Read these passages with your tween.

Have some fun with bread. You don't have to grind your own wheat to have a little fun with your family's daily bread. Here are three suggestions.

1. Talk about how Sunday is the Christian sabbath. Women in the days of Jesus baked double the amount of bread for the sabbath, because they were not to work on the sabbath and baking bread is work!

   Have the family work together to prepare for a real sabbath. On Saturday use your favorite bread recipe to teach your tween how to bake bread (yes, even the boys). Or you can always get prepared dough for bread or rolls and have your tween bake them in the oven. On this same weekend have all family members work together to clean the house, do all the laundry, and cook all food that will be eaten on Sunday. (Using the microwave on Sunday is acceptable.)

   Sunday, instead of doing a lot of chores, go to Sunday school and worship, then take the rest of the day off as a family—no work, no cooking. Take naps, go to the park, attend a ball game, or play a game; do whatever your favorite non-work thing to do as a family is.

   In other words, celebrate the sabbath.

2. Experience breads—For one month, each week (or a couple of times a week) experience as many different kinds of bread as possible. Make sure there are lots of breads you haven't eaten before (or that you do not eat very often). Eating a variety of breads is the key. Don't forget pita bread, matzoh (many local supermarkets carry it—it's unleavened bread), corn bread, tortillas, and so forth.

   At some point you might want to say the following: **If Jesus said "I am the bread of life," and there are so many varieties of bread, with bread meaning different things to different people, what could that mean?** (There are no pat answers here, just some things to speculate about. This is good for their brains as well as their souls.)

3. Start a tradition—Two nights a week have a "family meal" night. Every member of the family without exception sits down to eat together. No one is allowed to schedule anything to interfere with dinner on these nights.

Display Luminarias

In many stores these days you can purchase luminarias to line your walk with light. However, your tween can have a lot more fun by making his or her own to line your front porch or driveway. Here are two choices—paper bag luminarias or tin can luminarias.

Important: Make sure you closely watch any lit candles.

Paper Bag Luminaria

> *You will need: paper lunch bag, markers, sand, votive candle.*

1. Using felt-tip markers, decorate the outside of a paper lunch sack with Christian symbols (see the sketch).
2. Fold the top of the bag down twice to create a two- to three-inch collar.
3. Pour sand into the bottom of the sack (enough to make the sack stand up in place and to hold in drips from the candle).
4. Place a votive candle in the sand.

Tin Can Luminaria

> *You will need: tin can, water, hammer, nail, black paint, sand, votive candle.*

Fill tin cans (whatever size you have on hand, but the bigger the better) with water and freeze them. This gives the cans support during hammering and makes them much easier to work with.

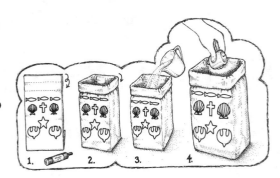

1. Use a nail and hammer to punch holes in the pattern of a decorative Christian symbol into the tin can. Run the cans under warm water to release the ice.
2. Paint the outside of the can with flat black paint. (Light shows through the pattern and can be seen much better if the paint is flat instead of glossy.)
3. Pour enough sand into the can to support a votive candle.
4. Place a votive candle in the middle of the can in the sand.

Have a Christian Christmas Tree

Decorate the family Christmas tree (or another tree) with only Christian ornaments this year. Choose from the many ornaments you probably already have on hand—things like stars, hearts (for love), candy canes (they represent the shepherd's staff), crosses, angels, and any of the many nativity ornaments now available. Be sure to use plenty of lights (Jesus is the light of the world). If you don't have enough of these ornaments on hand and are planing to buy new ornaments, why not make them ornaments with Christian symbolism?

You could also make chrismons or Christian ornaments. There are patterns with explanations in a number of books available through local Christian book stores.

Make a Family Prayer Candle

You will need: candle, straight pins, sequins, thimble.

Get a large, thick candle that will fit on a plate and sit comfortably in the middle of the family table. Give your tween the candle, straight pins, and gold or silver sequins. Give your tween a thimble, because it helps when pushing the pins into the hard wax.

Have your tween look at some of the symbols on this page; he or she may or may not want to use these symbols on the candle. Ask your tween to make symbols of some type that express Christianity or the church (besides those shown below they could create a Bible, a ship, a lamb, and so forth). Your tween may want to cut out the symbols and use them as a pattern if he or she does not feel able to make the symbol without a pattern.

Have your tween push the pins through the center of the sequins and then push the pin into the candle to form the design they have selected.

Whenever the family has a meal together light this prayer candle and say a blessing.

Together Through Holy Week

Your tween is at a time in life when he or she can come to a fuller appreciation of the joy of Easter morning if he or she experiences the sadness and grief that precedes this joyous occasion.

Holy Week is the most important season of the Christian church. Without the death and resurrection of Jesus Christ there would be no Christian church. Let Holy Week be more meaningful to all of you; worship together as often as possible this week.

Your church (or sometimes groups of churches in your area) hold many special services commemorating every event of Holy Week.

Palm Sunday—The joyful triumphal entry of Jesus into Jerusalem. A great and happy time.

Maundy (Holy) Thursday—This service commemorates the Last Supper of Jesus and the disciples. This is the time when the Lord's Supper was instituted and also the time that Jesus revealed the coming betrayal (by Judas) and denial (by Peter).

Good Friday Service—This service can be held at any time of the day on the Friday before Easter. It remembers the crucifixion and death of Jesus. Usually at this service the altar is stripped of all decorations. The cross is then usually draped in black to signify the death of Jesus. This service is a crucial service for setting the stage for Easter Sunday morning. If you cannot attend any other service together during the week, be sure to attend a Good Friday service together.

Tenebrae Service—This is a different and powerful kind of Good Friday service (or it can be part of the Maundy Thursday service). Tenebrae means "darkness"; this service is usually held in the evening. In this service fourteen candles and a Christ candle are lit. At the end of each section of the service, one candle is extinguished, leaving the church in darkness. The congregation leaves in silence.

Stations of the Cross—Many churches set up a stations of the cross that runs throughout Holy Week. Some set it up for only a set time (sometimes the Saturday before Easter). The stations follow Jesus' path through his arrest and trial. Each station deals with one aspect of this eventful day. This is often walked through in silence, with individuals reading the Scripture for themselves. Sometimes it is done in groups with a designated person at each station reading the Scripture.

Easter Sunrise Service—A service of celebration as the sun rises. This service is held at sunrise for that is when the women arrived at the empty tomb discovering the Resurrection.

Easter Service—A celebration of the Resurrection of Jesus Christ. The most important service of the Christian Year.

Look At Your Home Differently

As a family dedicate this week to looking at your home in a different way than you ever have before. (As a side benefit you could use this as a house-cleaning week and donate extra unused stuff to someplace like Goodwill Industries or the Salvation Army.)

1. Designate a container that you will put on top of or next to the most used item in your house—for example, the computer, the TV, or the microwave.

2. Together tour your home (take a pad and paper with you). In each room answer these questions. Is there anything on the floor or under the dressers, the bed, or the couch? Are things piled up anywhere? Why are these things there? Are you just messy? Have you run out of storage space in this room? Put a penny in the container for any item that you don't have a place to store properly in the room that it is in. If you are just messy, put in a quarter for each messy room in the house. (Dad, this includes the garage—but you just might want to make a general donation for the garage.)

3. Have every person in the family count how many pairs of shoes they have. For each pair of shoes that **have not** been worn **this week,** the person puts one penny in your container.

4. How many electronic/digital items do you have in each room of your house? (Include everything—computers, printers, TVs, radios, alarm clocks, dishwashers, refrigerators, small appliances, electric drills, electric screwdrivers, electronic games, pagers, cell phones, and so on. Don't forget that the thermostat is electric.) Discuss what your family would do if your electricity went out and there were no batteries at all. For every electronic/digital item in your house, put a nickel in the container. (You better have a lot of nickels on hand for this one.)

5. How many toilets do you have in your house? Talk about how there are places in the world that don't have indoor plumbing. Put a dime in your container for every toilet in your house.

6. After you have done the first five things on the list, then each family member must choose one thing for themselves that they really, really, really love, something that they use or wear a lot. Everyone must state what that something is and then agree **not** to wear or use it for **one full week**. Family members are to help keep each other honest. (No cheating on this—it must be something really hard to give up.)

7. At the end of the week have everyone discuss the question, "Do we love our stuff more than God and others?" This is a hard question and most of us are tempted to give a quick "yes" and then go on to our lives, or to answer, "no, we need all of these things for living today." Try to be honest as you struggle together for an answer about where your priorities lie. Remember it is not money, but "the love of money" which "is a root of all kinds of evil" (1 Timothy 6:10). The same with things. It's okay to have things; it's where your heart is that counts.

Family members can donate the money from this project to people in the U.S. who are homeless or who have lost everything in a fire or flood, or to people in another country who live in grinding poverty every day of their lives. Family members can also think of a way to earn money together (washing cars, mowing lawns, having a garage sale) to give to the selected charity.

Permission Slip for Field Trips

PROGRAM PERMISSION SLIP
For June 1, 20__ through May 31, 20__
Please return this completed form to the church office.

Youth Name:_____

Grade:_____   Age:_____

Address:_____
_____

E-mail:_____

Phone:_____   School:_____

School address:_____

School phone:_____

Allergies:_____

Other medical conditions:_____
_____

Parent(s) or guardian(s) name(s):_____

Home phone:_____   Work phone:_____

Cell phone:_____   Pager:_____

E-mail:_____

Please provide names of persons to contact if parent(s) or guardian(s) cannot be reached.

1. Name:_____   Home phone:_____
   Work phone:_____   Cell phone:_____
2. Name:_____   Home phone:_____
   Work phone:_____   Cell phone:_____
3. Name:_____   Home phone:_____
   Work phone:_____   Cell phone:_____

The above has my permission to participate on the _____ *[church name here]* _____ Church youth ministry events between June 1, 20__ and May 31, 20__. I also understand that _____ *[church name here]* _____ is not liable should injury come to my child. I give permission for emergency medical care to be given by a hospital should my child need such treatment before I am contacted.

Signature of parent or guardian:

_____

Insurance company and number: _____

Doctor's name:_____

Doctor's address:_____

Doctor's phone:_____

Other Resources

Check availability of these titles at your local Christian bookstore.

For Tweens

1. *My Journal: A Place to Write about God and Me* by Janet R. Knight and Lynn W. Gillian (Upper Room) 0835807916

2. *Hey, God, Let's Talk! Prayer Journal* by Chuck Terrell (Abingdon Press) 0687083516 (without music CD), 0687033799 (with music CD)

3. *Devozine*—A Devotional Magazine for Youth (Upper Room)
   Introduce this resource to older tweens. It is rather sophisticated for 10- and 11-year-olds.

4. *Dive Into Living Water: 50 Devotions for Teens on the Gospel of John* by Laurie Polich (Abingdon Press) 0687052238

5. *Closer to God Prayer Journal* (Abingdon Press) 0687068207

For Leaders

1. *Deepening Youth Spirituality: The Youth Worker's Guide* by Walt Marcum (Abingdon Press) 0687097258
   Look especially at the introduction.
   Caution: Do **not** assume that you can do everything with tweens that you can do with youth. Many tweens are still more concrete than abstract. Their attention span is also shorter.

2. *Out of the Box* edited by LeeDell Stickler (Abingdon Press) 0687092485
   See unit two: "Relating to God."

3. *Teaching Tips for Terrified Teachers* edited by Marcia Stoner (Abingdon Press) 0687084091
   See "Children in Worship" and "Relationships" sections.

4. *O Taste and See That the Lord Is Good* edited by LeeDell Stickler (Abingdon Press) 0687026067
   See "Planning the Worship" section.

5. *Helping Youth Pray: How to Connect Youth With God* by Greg McKinnon (Abingdon Press) 0687061903
   Some adaptation needed to use with tweens.

For Studies or Special Events

1. *Hey, God, Let's Talk* by Chuck Terrell (Abingdon Press) Teacher Book 0687033772
   Six-week study on prayer.

2. *Show Me the Way: 50 Bible Study Ideas for Youth* by Todd Outcalt (Abingdon Press) 068709562X
   This is basically a Bible study. Some activities are too old for tweens. But note page 31 ("Bible Worship"—shorten this activity for tweens), page 34 ("The Apostles' Creed"), and pages 41-45 ("The Bible Behind the Symbols"). May wish to make some modifications for those under 12.

3. *Signs of Faith: God's Word of Love* by Marcia Stoner (Abingdon Press) 0687099277
   Longer Bible verses in sign language for formal settings such as worship.

4. *Symbols of Faith: Teaching the Images of the Christian Faith* by Marcia Stoner (Abingdon Press) 0687094755
   Intergenerational; most activities may be used with tween or youth classes or groups.

5. *Worship Feast: 50 Complete Multi-Sensory Services for Youth* (Abingdon Press) 0687063671 (publication date is March 2003)
   Some adaptation needed to use with tweens.

6. *Worship Feast Ideas: 100 Awesome Ideas for Postmodern Youth* (Abingdon Press) 0687063574 (publication date is March 2003)
   Some adaptation needed to use with tweens.

7. *Tween Time: Fellowship and Service Projects for Preteens* (Abingdon Press) 0687022541 (publication date is May 2003)

Index

Index of Articles

Index of Activities

ARTS AND CRAFTS

BIBLE STUDY

BRAINSTORMING

COOKING

EVENTS

FAMILY ACTIVITIES

Credits

p. 123: Adapted from *Destination Unknown: 50 Quick Mystery Trips for Youth Groups*, copyright © 2001 Abingdon Press. Used by permission.

pp. 33, 66 (middle of page), 103 (top of page), 104 (top of page), 106 (top of page), 107: Adapted from *New Invitation: Grades 5–6*, Fall 1997, copyright © 1994, 1997 Cokesbury. Used by permission.

p. 119: Adapted from *New Invitation: Grades 5–6*, Winter 1997-98, copyright © 1994, 1997 Cokesbury. Used by permission.

p. 38: Adapted from *New Invitation: Grades 5–6*, Summer 1998, copyright © 1995, 1998 Cokesbury. Used by permission.

pp. 12 (top of page), 71, 120 (bottom of page): Adapted from *New Invitation: Grades 5–6*, Fall 1998, copyright © 1995, 1998 Cokesbury.

pp. 13, 15, 17 (top of page), 75 (bottom of page): Adapted from *New Invitation: Grades 5–6*, Winter 1998-99, copyright © 1995, 1998 Cokesbury. Used by permission.

pp. 22 (bottom of page), 88 (middle of page), 110: Adapted from *New Invitation: Grades 5–6*, Spring 1999, copyright © 1995, 1998 Cokesbury. Used by permission.

pp. 26, 63: Adapted from *New Invitation Grades 5-6*, Summer 1999, copyright © 1996, 1999 Cokesbury. Used by permission.

pp. 22 (top of page), 29, 52 (top of page): Adapted from *New Invitation: Grades 5–6*, Winter 1999-2000, copyright © 1995, 1999 Cokesbury. Used by permission.

pp. 16, 20 (bottom of page): Adapted from *New Invitation: Grades 5–6*, Spring 2000, copyright © 1996, 1999 Cokesbury. Used by permission.

pp. 9, 24 (bottom of page), 53 (bottom of page), 86 (bottom of page), 98 (bottom of page), 108 (bottom of page): Adapted from *Exploring Faith: Preteen*, Fall 2000, copyright © 2000 Cokesbury. Used by permission.

pp. 47 (Scripture references), 48-49: Adapted from *Exploring Faith: Older Elementary*, Winter 2000-2001, copyright © 2000 Cokesbury.

pp. 41, 45, 54, 55, 56, 65 (top of page), 68 (top of page), 89 (bottom of page), 90, 108 (top of page): Adapted from *Exploring Faith: Preteen*, Winter 2000-2001, copyright © 2000 Cokesbury. Used by permission.

pp. 82 (top of page), 85, 97: Adapted from *Exploring Faith, Older Elementary*, Spring 2001, copyright © 2000 Cokesbury.

pp. 34, 39 (bottom of page), 52 (bottom of page), 57 (bottom of page), 66 (top of page), 66 (bottom of page), 74, 81, 87, 91-94: Adapted from *Exploring Faith: Preteen*, Spring 2001, copyright © 2000 Cokesbury. Used by permission.

pp. 18, 24 (top of page), 27, 46: Adapted from *Exploring Faith: Preteen*, Summer 2001, copyright 2001 © Cokesbury. Used by permission.

pp. 21 (top of page), 105 (top of page): Adapted from *Exploring Faith: Older Elementary*, Fall 2001, copyright © 2001 Cokesbury. Used by permission.

pp. 35, 81: Adapted from *Exploring Faith: Preteen*, Fall 2001, copyright © 2001 Cokesbury. Used by permission.

pp. 114, 115: Adapted from *Exploring Faith With Families*, Fall 2001, copyright © 2001 Cokesbury. Used by permission.

pp. 99, 100 (top of page): Adapted from *Exploring Faith: Preteen*, Winter 2001–2002, copyright © 2001 Cokesbury. Used by permission.

pp. 10, 20 (top of page), 21 (bottom of page), 39 (top of page), 67, 76 (top of page), 106 (bottom of page): Adapted from *Exploring Faith: Older Elementary*, Spring 2002, copyright © 2001 Cokesbury. Used by permission.

pp. 30 (top of page), 42-43, 57 (top of page), 121, 122: Adapted from *Exploring Faith: Preteen*, Spring 2002, copyright © 2001 Cokesbury. Used by permission.

pp. 113: Adapted from *Exploring Faith With Families*, Spring 2002, copyright © 2001 Cokesbury. Used by permission.

pp. 19 (top of page), 72: Adapted from *Exploring Faith: Older Elementary*, Summer 2002, copyright © 2002 Cokesbury. Used by permission.

pp. 25 (bottom of page), 64: Adapted from *Exploring Faith, Preteen*, Summer 2002, copyright © 2002 Cokesbury Used by permission.

pp. 32, 61, 108 (top of page), 109 (top of page), 117 (top of page): Adapted from *Exploring Faith: Older Elementary*, Fall 2002, copyright © 2002 Cokesbury. Used by permission.

pp. 24 (top of page), 31 (top of page): Adapted from *Exploring Faith: Preteen*, Fall 2002, copyright © 2002 Cokesbury. Used by permission.

p. 116: Adapted from *Exploring Faith With Families*, Fall 2002, copyright © 2002 Cokesbury. Used by permission.

pp. 36, 79-80: Adapted from *Exploring Faith: Older Elementary*, Winter 2002-03, copyright © 2002 Cokesbury. Used by permission.

pp. 11 (bottom of page), 25 (top of page), 28, 30 (bottom of page), 37, 53 (top of page), 72, 75 (top of page), 76 (bottom of page), 77, 78, 98 (top of page), 109 (bottom of page): Adapted from *Exploring Faith: Preteen*, Winter 2002-03; copyright © 2002 Cokesbury. Used by permission.

pp. 14, 44, 105 (bottom of page): Adapted from *Exploring Faith: Preteen*, Spring 2003, copyright © 2002 Cokesbury. Used by permission.

pp. 50-51: Adapted from *Exploring Faith: Preteen*, lessons on journaling in 2000, 2001, and 2002, copyright © Cokesbury. Used by permission.